The Triangles of Management and Leadership

Copyright © 2002 Paul B. Thornton

All Rights Reserved

ISBN 1-59113-078-6

Published 2002

Published by Paul B. Thornton, USA. ©2002 Paul B. Thornton. All rights reserved. No part of this publication may be reproduced, stored in a retrieval system, or transmitted in any form or by any means, electronic, mechanical, recording or otherwise, without the prior written permission of the publisher.

Manufactured in the United States of America.

Booklocker.com, Inc.
2002

The Triangles of Management and Leadership

Paul B. Thornton

The Triangles of Management and Leadership

Dedication

**To Elizabeth Justine Bernadette Thornton
Thanks Mom!!**

Table of Contents

Acknowledgements 1
Introduction 3
Chapter 1 The Foundation: Mission, Vision and Values 5
Chapter 2 The Three Cs of Leadership 13
Chapter 3 The Big Three Management Styles 23
Chapter 4 Communications Triangle 31
Chapter 5 The Listening Triangle 41
Chapter 6 The Power Triangle 47
Chapter 7 Managing the Process 55
Chapter 8 The Three Phases of Planning 61
Chapter 9 Decision Making 69
Chapter 10 Three Approaches to Managing Conflict 77
Chapter 11 The ABCs of Motivation 85
Chapter 12 The Art of Giving Feedback 95
Chapter 13 The What, When, and How of Controls 103
Chapter 14 The Finance Triangle 109
Chapter 15 Dealing with Difficult People 119
Chapter 16 Introducing and Managing Change 127
Chapter 17 The Triangles of Leading Teams 135
Chapter 18 Managing Your Career 145

Bibliography 153
About the Author Paul B. Thornton 155

Acknowledgements

I am greatly indebted to Dr. Paul Hersey. He played a major role in the development and evolution of "Situational Leadership Theory." While at Ohio University I took his course on managing organizational behavior. It was my *best* college course. His passion and ability to teach stimulated my interest in management and leadership. He set me on a path I'm still excited to be on.

Most of the theories in this book are long-standing. I am greatly indebted to those who have educated me in these concepts. The "triangle concept" and anecdotes are new additions.

I appreciate all the consultants, managers, and leaders who provided examples of how they have applied the theory.

I would like to thank my family members.
- My wife, Mary Jean, for her insights and ideas about what makes effective managers and leaders. She has bullet-like focus and intense passion.
- My daughter, Kate, for proofreading and editing my manuscript. She's a wonderful person who has a special glow.
- My son, Andrew, for teaching me leadership lessons on the basketball court. He's an exceptional person and player.

Introduction

I just received a new book on management and leadership. It has 586 pages. Ouch!! Is management and leadership really that complex?

My goal is to simplify what you need to do to be an effective manager and leader. Jack Welch, former CEO of GE, has made the point that effective leaders are simple. They don't need a lot of clutter such as thick policy and procedure manuals.

The following 14 chapters are the core, nitty-gritty of what makes managers and leaders effective. Each topic is represented by a triangle. The triangle provides a visual reminder of the three critical variables that comprise each management/leadership concept. The three variables are interrelated. A change in one impacts the other two. Understanding these dynamic relationships is critical.

At times all employees are required to take on the role of manager and leader. What's the difference between manager and leader? The two roles have a lot of similarities but a few key differences. Leaders have visions of what could be. They energize and excite people to pursue bigger goals and bigger ideas. Managers do the

THE TRIANGLES OF MANAGEMENT AND LEADERSHIP

day-to-day planning, organizing, motivating, and decision making to achieve the vision.

I believe all employees have untapped abilities.

- You can lead.
- You can manage.
- You can make the difference.

Chapter 1
The Foundation: Mission, Vision and Values

What's our mission? Vision? Values?

Leaders find simple, clear and compelling answers to these questions. The answers have a profound influence on what employees think, say and do. These three building blocks—mission, vision and values—are vital to establishing an effective organization. Employees want to be part of an organization that has purpose, direction, and values, and offers meaningful work.

Mission
Our mission is to "make money." Satisfy the customer!" "Change the world!" A company's mission is a statement of its purpose or reason for being. Mission statements provide focus, inspiration and criteria to evaluate strategic choices. Here are some interesting comparisons of how organizations see their mission.

- Police Department: *"Our mission is to prevent crime." "Our mission is enforce the law."*

If the organization's mission is to "prevent crime" they're probably going to develop and implement educational programs. These efforts will be focused on helping people develop the knowledge and skills needed to manage conflict, handle stress and know the law. If the organization's mission is simply to "enforce the law" they will develop systems and procedures to catch people who violate the law.

- Airline: *"Our mission is to transport people from point A to Point B." "Our mission is to entertain people at 25,000 feet."*

Each purpose creates a very different company. In the first company employees are only concerned with efficiently transporting people. Employees at the second company are focused on entertaining passengers. "What can we do to make the trip enjoyable and memorable?"

- Manufacturer: *"Our mission is to make buggy whips." "Our mission is to design and produce leather products designed to satisfy customer needs."*

What if the company's mission is too narrow? Companies that said their mission was "to make buggy whips" no longer exist. On the other hand if a company said their mission was "to design and produce leather products" it could evolve and adapt as customers' needs changed.

I like Disney World's mission, *"to make people happy."* It's clear and succinct. All stakeholders—customers, employees, stockholders and the community—know what Disney is trying to accomplish.

Developing a focused and clear mission isn't easy. It often takes a lot of thinking and several iterations before it can be implemented. Your mission statement needs to be reviewed regularly to test its relevance to new conditions. Having a clear purpose is the first building block of success.

Vision
A vision statement describes a future state that's better in some important way than what currently exists. Business vision statements are challenging. They describe people and organizations not as they are, but as they can become.

A vision starts with what the leader really cares about and is fully committed to achieving. Margaret Thatcher said that it's the leader's responsibility to shine a spotlight on the future, then get the support of people to create that future.

Effective vision statements include the following characteristics:

- Inspiring—"*Our vision is to be the number one global supplier of hardware to the automotive industry.*" Will that vision inspire and motivate people to work 12- to 14-hour days? Maybe, but I don't think so. Vision statements need to connect with people at both the intellectual and the emotional level.
- Clear and vivid—Can you see it? Lillian started her weight loss program by putting a picture of herself, 30 pounds lighter, on the refrigerator. As the saying goes, "Seeing is believing." If you can see it or vividly picture it in your mind you have a much better chance of achieving it.
- A better future—What's to be gained? When change is occurring it's natural for people to focus on what they are giving up. Leaders have to help people see what's to be gained. People connect with a vision when they see the benefits. "WIIFM—What's in it for me? How is it going to make my life better?"

THE TRIANGLES OF MANAGEMENT AND LEADERSHIP

Vision describes your destination. Leaders must know what path they're on (their mission) and where it's taking them (their vision). When both mission and vision are clear, day-to-day issues and opportunities are seen within a larger context. The tasks of setting goals and priorities, planning, and implementation are aligned with the mission of the organization and its desired future. Effective leaders not only have a vision but also invest time selling their ideas and gaining buy-in.

Values

Leaders have to find answers to these questions: What are our values? What's important in this organization? How are we going to work together? These questions are important to an organization of 5 or 5000. Values are guiding principles that indicate what behaviors are needed for success and what behaviors are unacceptable.

Harley Davidson describes their values as follows:

- Tell the truth
- Be fair
- Keep your promises
- Respect the individual
- Encourage intellectual curiosity

If you worked at Harley Davidson you'd be expected to tell the truth and keep your promises. Some companies put their values on a plastic card and give one to every employee. That's fine, but "values" need to be visible—practiced and modeled. Employees observe leaders to see if their actions match their words. If there is a gap, credibility is lessened or lost.

Two of GE's values are the following:

- Have a passion for excellence and hate bureaucracy.
- Have enormous energy and the ability to energize others.

Certainly Jack Welch, GE's leader for the past ten years, sets the example for each of these values. That makes them real and believed by the organization.

Some teams develop "operating rules" (values) which define how team members will work together. One team I was on developed the following operating rules:

- Begin and end meetings on time
- Listen, no interruptions
- Active participation is required
- Decisions by consensus
- Be prepared, complete assigned action items

These rules established an expectation of how we would behave. Were the rules always followed? No. What happened if a team member violated one of the rules? In high performing teams all members hold each other accountable to following the rules.

Every major religion has a set of rules for members to follow. In a similar way leaders have to establish values, guiding principles, or operating rules to define what's important and how people will work together. Leaders demonstrate their values in their actions and behaviors. Kim Krisco, author of *Leadership Your Way*, says that communicating a list of values before they are reflected in tangible ways can turn values into hollow words.

THE TRIANGLES OF MANAGEMENT AND LEADERSHIP

Summary

Mission, vision and values are three important pieces of the puzzle. Without mission, there's no purpose. Without vision, there's no destination. Without values, there are no guiding principles. When mission, vision and values aren't clear, it's easy to lose focus, get off track, and pursue the wrong goals.

Effective leaders make sure all employees understand and support the organization's core beliefs. On a daily basis, leaders demonstrate their commitment to these building blocks. When strategic options and difficult problems arise, leaders ask questions such as:

- Does this align with our mission?
- Is this action in line with our vision?
- Are we adhering to our values?

Applying the Concept

Dave Logan, President, Palmer Foundry

I look at vision as the dream we all need. Dreams are what make life exciting and interesting. During the past year, our business suffered a catastrophic loss due to a massive fire. Much of the plant was destroyed. Everything looked like a mess, felt like a mess, and it was very difficult to see beyond the rubble. We needed a vision. We needed a positive picture of the future to buoy our spirits as we argued with the insurance company, dealt with concerned customers, and slowly rebuilt our business. We faced many investment decisions as we rebuilt. Knowing what type of product we wanted to make and the type of customer we wanted to serve guided us during the reconstruction process. With so many decisions to make, having a focused vision kept our team pulling in the same direction.

Our mission helps clarify why we exist. In our case, we don't want to have the largest share for all aluminum castings. We want to be the premier source for aluminum castings that have unique engineering challenges. We want our employees to know what type of work we are going to pursue. When we decline high volume–low quality work, our employees know why.

Sharing core values makes life much easier. There is less confusion, and everyone knows the type of people we want on our team as we pursue our dreams. Honesty is one of our key values. As a leader, be honest with yourself and your employees. I often hear company leaders say they want to be the biggest and best in their industry. Bigger isn't always better, and not everyone needs to be a worldwide leader. Pursue a vision and mission that really captures the essence of what you want your company to be. Don't look at the mission, vision, values exercise as a PR gimmick. It's important stuff.

Applying the Concept

**Jamie Walters, Founder and President, Ivy Sea
(Communication and Leadership Consultants)**

Closing the gap between the espoused mission and vision, and the reality that is lived day-to-day in the organization, is key. At Ivy Sea, and with our clients, we do an in-depth review of the vision and mission annually. We've created a specific process called the Ivy Sea Visioning Model. Part of the annual vision review includes *a no-excuses look at what the words of the vision and mission really mean. We explore what the words or jargon look, sound and feel like on an average day in the company. How do customers experience that? What does that mean for how people interact within the organization? What are each individual's responsibilities to the organization? What can he or she expect back from the organization?*

Too often, a visioning program results in a vague statement that is never connected to everyday actions and experiences, which takes the power out of the vision and is likely to generate cynicism from employees and customers.

After the annual vision reviews, we get together on a quarterly basis to talk about how and where the vision was put into action, and where opportunities exist to do so in the coming months.

This same approach, once the "vision in action" is defined, permeates job descriptions, performance expectations and performance reviews. All company communications reinforce the connection between the lofty vision language and the everyday activities, including examples of how specific employees performed in a way that supported the vision. Each role is connected to implementing the vision, as are expectations, and performance is evaluated based on how, specifically, each individual contributed in support of the vision and mission.

This way, regardless of what's happening in the larger economy or the normal cycles of business, we're always grounded in our vision and what that means for us each day, week, month and quarter. We understand it so well that we can easily evaluate opportunities and decisions to ensure they're truly aligned with what we're here to do. We encourage and assist our clients in doing the same.

Chapter 2
The Three Cs of Leadership

The Army's motto—"Be All That You Can Be" is both simple and powerful. Leaders help people achieve that goal. In essence, leaders do three things:

- They challenge people.
- They build people's confidence.
- They coach people.

By providing the right "C" (challenge, confidence, or coaching), leaders help people become more and achieve more than they thought possible.

The three Cs are interrelated. As leaders coach and mentor people, they feel more prepared, more confident. As confidence increases, people are more willing to take on bigger and bigger challenges. Sue Lewis, executive vice president and chief real estate officer, The Travelers, asserts, "Many leaders are good at only one or two Cs but not all three. In today's business world challenge is common. However, coaching and building confidence are frequently missing."

Desire to Lead

What gives people the desire to lead? People's values and beliefs are often shaped by significant emotional events. These defining moments energize some people to take a stand against injustice or pursue a new standard of excellence. In other instances, the desire to lead is sparked by a compelling vision. "My vision gets me excited. My adrenaline starts pumping." Desire to lead may be generated simply by the desire to help others grow and blossom. An executive states, "Somewhere along the way I learned it was very exciting and rewarding to help other people achieve their dreams. That's what leaders do."

If a person lacks that desire, he or she will not take on a leadership role. Charlie Eitel, former president and COO, Interface, Inc., states, "To want to be the leader is to risk failure. I'm convinced that everyone is afraid to fail — it's a matter of degree. Fear is what causes people to play not to lose." On the other hand, seeing what is possible and playing to win is exciting and energizing.

Challenging People

Actress Cicely Tyson says that challenges make you discover aspects of yourself that you never knew existed. Challenges are what make people stretch and go beyond the norm. Leaders use many of the following approaches to challenge people and change the status quo:

- **Describing their vision**—Every leader has one. Visions describe a future that's better in some important way. A clear and compelling vision challenges people to think and act differently as they pursue a new agenda.
- **Establishing stretch goals**—When Richard Davis became CEO of Rand McNally, the company launched an average of ten new products per year. He challenged the organization to

launch 120 new products during his first year. Nothing commands people's attention like demanding targets and timetables.
- **Asking provocative questions**—Leaders often ask "why" and "what if" questions. The right questions force people to examine underlying assumptions and consider new possibilities. Stuart Hornery, retired chairman, Lend Lease Corporation, states, "Every project we take starts with a question-- how can we do what's never been done before?"
- **Benchmarking**—Ayn LaPlant, president, Beekley Corporation, states, "Benchmarking is another way we challenge people. I want our employees to look at other companies and find best practices. If you're really committed to continuous improvement, you have a natural curiosity to learn from the best."
- **New assignments**—Ruth Branson, senior vice president, Shaw's Supermarkets, states, "We challenge people through cross-fertilization. We move people into new positions, from one function to another, from line to staff, from a district to the corporate office. These job changes stretch people to see the business from new perspectives."

All of these leadership actions—stating your vision, establishing stretch goals, asking tough questions, benchmarking and new assignments—challenge people to see bigger possibilities and pursue bigger goals. Leaders also set the example by challenging themselves. If the leader isn't getting out of his comfort zone, it's unlikely others will follow.

Building Confidence
Confident people face their challenges. They're willing to leave their comfort zone, take risks, and try new approaches. People who

lack confidence want to keep doing things the same old way. Jan Carlson, the legendary CEO of Scandinavian Airline Systems(SAS), believes the most important role for a leader is to instill confidence in people. Even after people develop self-confidence they can lose it. Leaders use a variety of techniques to build people's confidence, including the following:

- **Affirm people's talents**—Don Sweet, vice-president, finance, Siebe Pneumatics, says, "People need self-confidence or belief in themselves so that they can perform with the best. I sometimes simply affirm my confidence in people. For example, one of our sales reps was facing a new, very demanding account. I said to him, 'I know you can do this. I know you can get through to this client.'"
- **Rewarding and recognizing accomplishments**—Real confidence is based on achieving results, one success after another. When leaders provide rewards and recognition, it's a validation of people's talents and determination.
- **Training and development**—Bill Cox, vice president, human resources, Ahlstrom Corporation, states, "We build people's confidence by making sure all employees receive ongoing training. One of our key beliefs is that competence builds confidence."
- **Empower people**—Ralph Stayer, former CEO of Johnsonville Foods, built confidence in his workforce by transferring total responsibility and ownership to the people doing the work. When leaders give people responsibility and real authority, they're saying, "I have confidence in you."
- **Remind people of their previous successes**—Sometimes people forget or overlook their previous successes. Jim Ligotti, former global product manager, Carrier Corporation remarks, "When challenges seem overwhelming or when people are reluctant to change, I go back to their successes in non-work

related areas. I remind people that they did achieve success in other areas of their life."

All of these leadership actions—affirming people, recognizing accomplishments, skills training, empowering people, and reminding them of previous successes—have a significant impact on people's self-confidence. Confident people face reality and have a "can do" attitude. Leaders also need a healthy amount of their own self-confidence. Confident leaders aren't afraid to attack "sacred cows," make tough decisions, and candidly communicate their positions.

Coaching

Coaching is all about raising people's performance to a higher level. Before people are open to coaching, they need to understand why they need to improve. That's the challenge. Secondly, they need to believe they are capable of changing. That's the confidence factor. Coaching involves the "how-to-do-it" part of the equation.

Steve Chanin, director, operations, ABB Corp., believes coaching involves helping people understand the big picture. People need to understand the key business drivers, what they can control, and what's important to the customer. Leaders use a variety of approaches to coach people, including the following:

- **Create coaching opportunities**—Take the time to carefully observe people as they run meetings, make presentations, and interact with customers. Dan Kelly, vice president, transportation business, International Fuel Cells, gives his direct reports frequent opportunities to make presentations. He states, "These can be emotional events and powerful learning opportunities." Leaders look for "teachable moments" when people are most open to learning.

- **Show them what great performance looks like**—Top leaders are constantly searching for best practices and great performance in all aspects of business. Encouraging others to observe and study what top performers do and don't do is an excellent coaching technique.
- **Ask questions**—Socrates' basic method of teaching was asking questions. The right questions help people focus on the areas needing improvement. Leaders spend time identifying the best questions to ask such as: "What question will help this person face reality?" "What question will energize this person?" "What question will help this individual identify specific next steps to be taken?"
- **Provide feedback**—Michael Z. Kay, president and CEO, LSG Sky Chefs, Inc., states, "Give frequent, candid feedback. Let people know where they are strong but also where they need to improve. Always demonstrate your confidence in people's ability to learn and grow." He also believes in establishing rigorous consequences for not taking risks and trying new ways of getting things done.
- **Set the example**—Great coaches are usually great students. They keep learning and growing throughout their lives. Janice Deskus, vice president, training and quality implementation, CIGNA Health Care, states, "Every meeting I attend, I try to walk away with at least one new idea."

Coaches help athletes develop the required skills and mind-set needed to excel in their sport. In a similar way, leaders coach and help people achieve their best performance. These coaching actions—pointing out examples of top performance, asking the right questions, providing helpful feedback and setting a positive example—help people develop the knowledge and skills needed to succeed. Leaders view every coaching event as an opportunity to gain new insights about themselves and their associates.

Summary

Leaders have the desire to help people "be all they can be." They use the right amount of each C (challenge, confidence, and coaching) to help people stretch, believe in themselves, and develop new skills.

In the book *Jesus, CEO: Using Ancient Wisdom for Visionary Leadership*, author Laurie Beth Jones states that Jesus was a great leader and would have made a great CEO. What specific actions did Jesus take?

1. He challenged people. He challenged his 12 recruits to give up their current jobs and take on a bigger and more meaningful task. He challenged people to think morally and act ethically.
2. He built confidence. He believed in his recruits. He saw great potential in each of them. When they failed he didn't judge them—rather he encouraged them to keep trying.
3. He coached. He believed his role was to help and nurture others. There are countless stories of Jesus teaching and preaching wherever he went. He trained his staff so effectively that they continued to do the work after his death.

Leaders provide the challenge, confidence, and coaching people need to achieve their best performance.

Applying the Concept

Sue Lewis, Executive Vice President and Chief Real Estate Officer, The Travelers

Each person and team is unique and has its own set of needs. There is no one leadership approach that fits all situations. Many leaders are good at one or two of the Cs but not all three. In today's business world, challenge is common. What's often missing is coaching and building confidence to help people face the challenge.

Regarding challenge, I look for ways to push people out of their comfort zone, but not in a way that will paralyze them. Like throwing a rock in a pond, I try to stretch people one ripple at a time. When challenges are given, I provide people with a backdrop to put the goal in context. People want to know why their company cares about this particular goal and why they should care. I also find it helpful to describe what it will be like a year from now if we accomplish the objective. Once challenges are in place, I periodically check in with people to see what's happening. What obstacles are they facing? What's working and not working? This gives me insight in terms of what I need to do in the areas of confidence building and coaching. People need confidence to take risks. They also need to know what happens if they don't achieve the improvement target. A key lesson I've learned is that I need to set the example. No one will stretch more than I do. In addition I have to demonstrate self-confidence to take risks and try radical approaches if necessary.

Leaders need to develop their own styles and approaches to each of the Cs. It's not enough just to challenge people. Accomplished business leaders are comfortable taking risks and performing at the top of their game. However, many people need coaching to develop the skills and mind-set to compete with the best. Effective leaders help people achieve their potential by engaging in all three Cs.

Applying the Concept

Dan Kelly, Vice President, Transportation Business, International Fuel Cells

I get a great deal of satisfaction helping people develop. You have to be willing to challenge people and hold them accountable for results. People who only want to be buddies with everyone won't challenge people or give them candid feedback.

I try not to prejudge people in terms of what they can or can't accomplish. I've been very surprised and pleased at what some people have accomplished. I try to set clear expectations and support people as required. However, before people accept a tough challenge, they need self-confidence. They need to believe they can succeed.

Before I can build someone's confidence, I need to trust him. When we establish project expectations, I try to weave into the conversation that the person has the talents and abilities to be successful. But it's more than just words. It's the trust I have in them and the way I deliver the message that shows my confidence. I also tell people that if they make a mistake I will support their decisions. I try never to attack people for making decisions. That creates fear and that leads to inaction, which is unacceptable.

THE TRIANGLES OF MANAGEMENT AND LEADERSHIP

A lot of leaders don't provide effective coaching. They simply pass on customer demands, which are often the tough challenges. Without confidence and coaching people flounder. I coach people at our weekly meetings. I'm very willing to discuss and provide guidance. I want to hear people's ideas. Coaching often involves helping people learn new ways to see a problem and all the impacts of their recommendations.

I also give people frequent opportunities to make presentations to customers and senior management. These are powerful learning opportunities. After the presentation we discuss what was positive and negative. People appreciate the feedback. A key part of my job is encouraging people to try new, hopefully more effective ways of communicating their ideas.

Leaders must have confidence in themselves. They must believe in their vision and show people how committed they are to achieving it. If I don't set the example, I lack credibility. Without credibility, I won't be effective at challenging people, building their confidence, or coaching them.

Chapter 3
The Big Three Management Styles

Management literature describes numerous management styles, including assertive, autocratic, coaching, country club, directing, delegating, laissez faire, participatory, supportive, task oriented and team-based. Are there really that many styles? I believe there are three basic styles—directing, discussing and delegating, **The 3-Ds of Management Style**. The appropriate style provides the right amount of structure and support for each situation. Each style is unique in terms of how managers communicate, set goals, make decisions, monitor progress and recognize good performance.

Directing Style
Managers tell people what to do, how to do it and when to have it completed. They assign roles and responsibilities, set standards and define expectations.

- **Communications**—The manager speaks, employees listen and react. Managers provide detailed instructions so employees know exactly what to do. The ability to communicate in a clear, concise, and complete fashion is critical. The only feedback managers ask for is, "Do you understand what needs to be done?"

- **Goal-Setting**—"Your goal is to sell 15 cars per month." The manager establishes short-term goals. When goals are specific and time bounded, employees are clear on what is expected of them. Goals and deadlines often motivate people.
- **Decision-Making**—"I want you to stop what you are currently doing and help Sue set up the room for the seminar." The manager makes most if not all decisions. When problems arise the manager evaluates options, makes decisions and directs employees as to what actions to take.
- **Monitoring Performance and Providing Feedback**— Managers establish specific control points to monitor performance. "Get back to me at 11:00 a.m. to brief me on what you've accomplished." Managers provide frequent feedback including specific instructions on how to improve performance.
- **Rewards and Recognition**—What makes a "directing style" manager happy? When people follow directions. "Great job, you did exactly what I told you to do."

The directing style is appropriate when there is a mandate from above that describes *what* must be done and *how* it must be done. The manager is the "commander in charge" simply carrying out the orders. The directing style is also appropriate when employees have limited experience or lack the skills needed to complete the assignment. Directing style managers provide the structure, action steps and controls necessary to complete the task.

Discussing Style

Managers using this style take time to discuss relevant business issues. What happens in a good discussion? People present ideas, ask questions, listen, provide feedback, challenge assumptions and coach as needed. It's important to make sure ideas are fully discussed and debated. Managers often perform the role of facilitator, making sure the discussion stays on track and everyone has a chance to contribute.

- **Communication**—Two-way communication is the norm. "Let's go around the table and give everyone a chance to discuss their ideas." Managers spend as much time asking questions and listening as they do talking and sharing their ideas. The right question focuses the discussion and draws out people's ideas.
- **Goal-Setting**—"Ingrid, what do you think our sales target should be for the fourth quarter?" After adequate discussion, goals are established. Utilizing a participatory style generally increases employees' commitment to achieve their goals.
- **Decision-Making**—"We have a problem with the amount of inventory we're currently carrying. What action do you think we should take?" Decisions are made collaboratively. Both manager and employee play an active role in defining problems, evaluating options, and making decisions.
- **Monitoring Performance and Providing Feedback**—The manager and employee monitor performance and discuss what actions need to be taken. This works best when both parties are open and make adjustments as needed.
- **Rewards and Recognition**—"Jason, you make an excellent point about the proposed organizational structure." Managers recognize people when they contribute to the discussion, ask good questions, build on the ideas of others, and are open to new ideas.

The discussion style is appropriate when there are opportunities to influence answers to questions such as, "What are our goals?" "What quality standards are needed?" "What work process should be used?" Who should do the work?" "What type of controls and feedback are needed?" The discussion style is effective when employees have ideas and confidence to speak up. Involvement in determining *what* must be done and *how* it will be done increases employees' commitment to making it happen.

Delegating Style
Managers using this style usually explain or get agreement on *what* has to be accomplished and *when* it must be completed. The *how-to-do-it* part of the equation is left up to the employee. Responsibility and authority are given to employees to get the job done.

- **Communications**—Regarding *what* has to be accomplished, communications may be one-way: "I want you to deliver a 15-minute presentation on our new compensation program at Tuesday's meeting." In other situations it may be two-way: "Let's discuss what needs to be accomplished in the marketing brochure you're designing." Additional communication takes place to review what has been accomplished and obstacles preventing progress.
- **Goal-Setting**—As stated above, specific goals may be established by the manager or may evolve after a discussion between manager and employee. Failures in delegation can often be traced back to a lack of understanding of the desired output or deliverable. "I thought you only wanted recommendations, not an implementation plan."
- **Decision-Making**—"Barbara, that's your decision to make." Decisions as to how the task will be accomplished are left to the employee. Employees have the power to take appropriate actions to achieve the desired goals. Managers must avoid "reverse delegation" when employees try to give back decisions that they should be making.
- **Monitoring Performance and Providing Feedback**—"I want a weekly update on plan accomplishments." Managers decide

how much monitoring is necessary. The amount of monitoring depends on the priority of the task and the person doing it. Providing feedback is the responsibility of the employee. Keeping the manager informed, especially when the plan is off track, is critical.
- **Rewards and Recognition**—Managers reward and recognize people who demonstrate the ability to work independently, make decisions and get the job done. "Helen, you worked through numerous obstacles. You found a way to make it happen. Great job!"

The delegating style is appropriate when people have the knowledge, skills and motivation to get the job done. Experienced people don't need a manager telling them what to do. They want the freedom to choose how to get the work done. This style gives managers more time to spend on other tasks such as benchmarking, strategic thinking and planning.

Summary
Each style (directing, discussing, and delegating) is unique in terms of how the management functions are executed. One senior executive states, " I often use a hybrid approach. I'll use a directing style on *what* needs to be accomplished and a discussing style to determine *how* it should be done. Other times after a good discussion, I'll delegate. I tell my associate it's his or her decision to decide how to proceed." Effective managers use all three management styles to work with and through people to achieve organizational goals. The appropriate **3-D style** challenges and motivates people to achieve the desired results.

Applying the Concept

Susan Fowler, Division Manager, Business Services, Norwich Public Utilities

My most natural style is discussing and generally that works well with the supervisory/management people that report directly to me. I have found, however, that I often end up using all three styles, depending on the subject matter, with the very same people.

For example, one person on my staff is a highly qualified technical manager to whom I have delegated most technical decisions with little input from me (e. g., budget constraints); however, he does not communicate well with his customers. This weakness results in complaints about his timeliness and ability to keep the customer up-to-date. In this area, I use the directing style to tell him what, when, and how to negotiate deadlines and keep his customer informed of progress. On another topic, employee development, this same manager and I are in discussing mode. We set performance goals, agree on development assignments for the staff, and assess progress as a team.

I use two basic clues to determine when to use each management style. The degree to which the outcome of using the style meets the objectives, and how the employee feels about the style are both important.

Usually, after making one or two assignments, I can tell whether the person has the necessary skills, judgment, and resources needed to be successful. With new employees I start with the discussing style and move in either direction as needed.

Sometimes even though an employee can and is successful, he or she needs more than the "textbook" amount of guidance. I once had two highly competent people working in similar roles who needed very different styles. One did her thing and kept me informed. She used me to bounce ideas off, but never waited for or expected approval before proceeding. She gave me reports and I rarely checked on progress. The other person, who was equally competent but less experienced, felt that I didn't care about his work unless I checked on progress frequently and provided feedback on how he was proceeding. At first I didn't know my delegating style with him was ineffective because he was meeting objectives. On the other hand, he always seemed to want to stop by and give me verbal updates that I felt were unnecessary. Finally I asked him how our relationship was working for him and he told me how he felt about my lack of apparent interest. He thought what he was doing was not important unless I was asking about the progress on a regular basis. What I thought was a vote of confidence was actually eroding his confidence.

When using each style it's important to pay attention to both project results and the behavior/morale of the people. If both are good, keep doing what you're doing. If not, ask questions and make adjustments.

Chapter 4
Communications Triangle

Only effective communication achieves the desired results!

Communication breakdowns lead to problems in quality, cost, and customer satisfaction. As one of my previous bosses used to say, "There's a cost to confusion." Managers and leaders must have the ability to communicate their ideas clearly, concisely and completely. The following basics are important for effective communication.

Know your purpose—What are you trying to accomplish? What do you want the receiver to know, think or do? Some managers make the mistake of thinking that a message will sound fresher and more interesting if they just "wing it." The result can be a pointless ramble—leaving the listener walking away scratching her head.

Word choice—Use words that are simple and precise. Words like "big," "small," and "later" are simple but imprecise. "Have it completed by 10:00 a.m. tomorrow" will produce better results than "Have it completed as soon as possible." Also, be careful when using jargon. Many employees may not understand certain technical lingo and specialized words.

Provide an overview—"I want to make three points." The overview provides the receiver with a roadmap of where you're going and the stops you will make along the way. An overview informs the receiver of how many mental files to set up to organize the information presented.

Organize the message—Just as it is difficult to find what you need in a messy desk drawer, it's hard to find meaning in a disorganized message. As a general rule, it's best to move from the big picture to progressively more detailed information. In addition, the discussion should lead to a clearly stated conclusion.

Channel—There are a number of ways to transmit a message, including phone, conference call, face to face, e-mail, group-meeting, and written memos. Each channel has advantages and disadvantages. It's important to consider how much information needs to be communicated and how quickly, how many people make up your audience, and how important it is to have real time interaction with the receiver.

Deliver the message—Make eye contact. "Look at me when I talk to you" is the frustration of every parent, teacher and coach. Use gestures. Effective communicators use gestures as visual aids to help explain their ideas and emotions. Use pauses. "Take a moment and think about that." Pauses can help emphasize key ideas and provide a transition to a new topic.

Motivate the listener—Let the receiver know what is in it for them. How will this information help them? Let's be realistic; people's attention does wander. Summon it back with words that signal the listener to focus and pay close attention: "Listen carefully to these instructions…," "The most important point to remember is…"

Great communicators are also effective at using the communications triangle, which includes:

- Painting pictures
- Telling stories
- Providing dramatic contrast

Paint Pictures
The best communicators paint pictures. They use colorful language to describe what it looks like and feels like. For example, "The red BMW convertible" is easy to visualize. Former President Ronald Reagan once said, "…a trillion bucks amounts to a stack of dough as high as the Empire State Building." Many managers and leaders use picturesque phrases like the following:

- The train has left the station
- Peel back the onion
- The wheels are off the wagon
- Like a dog shakes off water
- The ball is in your court
- Pull the trigger

If the receiver can visualize what is being said, it's more likely he will stay tuned. In addition, when leaders paint pictures, it creates interest and conveys information in a way that makes it more memorable.

Tell Stories
Dr. Howard Gardner says that the ability to tell stories constitutes the single most powerful weapon in a leader's arsenal. Why is that? Stories hold people's attention and interest. They build

suspense because we're not sure what the ending will be. A former vice president states, "Stories are about real people, real issues and real conclusions. People identify with the situation because they have faced similar problems."

Good stories are simple and easy to follow. A senior executive states, "The best stories are personal. They describe how people faced difficulty, struggled personally, experienced doubt and found a way to succeed." A student in my organizational behavior class relayed the following story:
"My husband died a few years ago. I was left with two teenage children and a business to run that I knew nothing about. I had doubts, fears and anxious moments. Somehow I found the courage to carry on. I survived and prospered. Today, I have two great kids and I run a successfull business." Great story with a great message.

Managers and leaders often use stories to make a point about customer service, on-time delivery, teamwork and quality. Here are some lead-ins to stories.

- "Last week I went to see my son's college basketball team play. The five players on the court ..."
- "Yesterday, I was at lunch with some friends. I asked the waitress if I could have a just a half sandwich and a cup of soup. She said, "That's not on the menu but..."
- "I decided to install a new garage door opener. I started reading the manual. It was 12 pages long, small print and very confusing. On page three I ..."

The ability to tell stories that people can relate to is an effective communication tool.

Provide Dramatic Contrast
Managers and leaders often provide a dramatic contrast between good and bad, right versus wrong, changing and not changing. By contrasting, managers and leaders simplify the issue and help people understand what must be done and why. Here are a few examples:

- "We need to get the right people on the team and the wrong people off the team."
- "Our choice is to embrace risk and uncertainty as a challenge. Or stay in our comfort zone and lose market share."
- "...transition from manager as order giver to manager as facilitator."
- "Leaders must know when to hold and when to fold—the leader must know what battles to fight."

Interrelationships
Ross Perot founded and built Electronic Data Systems (EDS) into a multi-billion dollar corporation employing more than 70,000 people. In 1984, he sold EDS to General Motors. He became GM's largest stockholder and a member of the board of directors. After a short tenure on the board he told the following story to describe the differences between EDS and GM.

What happens when you see a poisonous snake? The first EDS'er, who sees it, kills it. At GM, the first thing they do is form a committee on snakes. Second, they hire a consultant who knows a lot about snakes. Third, they sit around and discuss snakes for a year.

Using about 50 words, Perot hit all parts of the communication triangle. He paints a vivid picture, tells a great story, and makes a sharp contrast between EDS and GM.

THE TRIANGLES OF MANAGEMENT AND LEADERSHIP

Summary
The ability to communication ideas clearly, concisely and completely is vital for being an effective manager and leader. What does it take? Preparation. Know your purpose. Organize your ideas. Provide a roadmap. Make eye contact. Use gestures. Paint pictures. Tell good stories. It takes a lot to be a great communicator.

Applying the Concept

Kare Anderson, Emmy Winner, former Wall Street Journal Reporter and "Say It Better" Speaker

To be an effective communicator I try to do the following:

1. *Become clear about my main goal or need in my interaction with another person.*
2. *Attempt to understand the other person's main goal or need.*
3. *Then consider how to initiate communication with that person, based on their main need. Those considerations include the subject, language, tone, style and body language that I might use to make a genuine connection to that person.*
4. *The goal is to show a genuine awareness of the other person's interests. To do so, communicate, using the "You-Us-Me" approach. First (You) address the other person's interests, then (Us) relate it to what you share in common, then (Me) refer to how it relates to your interests. More effective than the frequently used form of communication, "Me—You", the research shows that when you "You-Us-Me", people listen*

sooner, longer and believe you are committed to serving their interests, too.
5. To become more credible and memorable, start communication with a specific detail, rather than general background information. People are more likely to listen sooner and longer. The specific detail proves the general conclusion.
6. To help others remember what you say, offer vivid contrasts such as a best and worst case scenario, an example from the world, or startling statistic. In your stories, involve the universally expressed emotions which include love, humor, anger, sadness, fear or disgust or inspiration.
7. Show respect for the other person with whom you want to communicate. When addressing someone indicate upfront:
    a.) why what you are saying might be of interest to them,
    b.) what you expect from them in the communication (for them to make a choice, be informed, consider something for future decision making,) and
    c.) about how much of their time you wish to take in the conversation.

In a time-starved, increasingly transient and relationship-diminished world, the most compelling, trusted communicators are those who demonstrate an awareness of others' needs, a capacity to communicate to create mutually beneficial relationships, and a commitment to making and keeping agreements that serve those mutual interests.

Applying the Concept

Jack O'Neill, Public Relations Advisor, Springfield Technical Community College and longtime Radio/TV Broadcaster

I learned some time ago that just because I sat in front of a microphone and/or television camera, it didn't make me a good communicator. Some of the things I've learned about being an effective communicator include:

- *Get people "involved" in what you're saying. Writing techniques for the broadcast media attempt to involve the listener/viewer. For example, it's better to say, "Your morning commute might have been longer today if you were on the South End Bridge," as opposed to, "There was an accident on the South End Bridge."*
- *The present tense is the most engaging form of communication. People are most engaged in the "here and now"—present moment.*
- *Credibility is key. It doesn't take long for people to either believe or not believe what you say. When Ronald Reagan, in a calm, quiet voice, told air traffic controllers that if they did not return to work they would be fired, he backed it up by firing them. Whether or not you agreed with the action, you believed that Reagan meant what he said from that moment on.*
- *Don't overwhelm people with too many ideas and concepts, because like a bucket of water dumped on you, most of it will run off. Few people can absorb 10 new ideas all at once or make dramatic changes overnight.*
- *You communicate with your eyes and ears before you use the written or spoken word. When I speak to a group, the first thing I try to determine is the mood and energy of the group.*

Observe people. Listen for their hopes and dreams as well as their frustrations and fears.
- *Email has certainly changed communications. People perceive things differently when they are written as opposed to verbalized. What's funny when spoken can take on a very different meaning when sent through cyberspace. Care should be taken and thought given to any form of communication prior to sending the message.*

Like golf, being an effective communicator requires ongoing practice, feedback, and reflection.

Chapter 5
The Listening Triangle

"I can't hear you!
"Your body language indicates boredom."
"What do you mean by a 'significant increase?'"

Dr. Mitchell Rabkin, CEO, Beth Israel Hospital in Boston, has a small figurine of a little boy on his desk. The child is squatting, picking up something, and looking it over. Dr. Rabkin says that the statue is there to remind people of how important it is for everyone to be curious without any preconceptions. Asking questions, listening and learning are important activities for every manager and leader.

People feel valued and appreciated when you truly listen to their ideas. Dr Tony Alessandra, keynote speaker and author of *The Platinum Rule* states, "I treat every conversation as an opportunity to gain that one piece of information that will give me the edge. The edge in terms of understanding people, connecting with them, and being able to lead them in more effective ways." The best listeners are genuinely curious. They want to know *what* people think and *how* they arrived at their conclusions.

THE TRIANGLES OF MANAGEMENT AND LEADERSHIP

The listening triangle involves the following:

- Understanding purpose
- Hearing the words
- Observing body language

Understanding purpose
What's the speaker's purpose or objective? Is it sharing information, problem solving, soliciting opinions or something else? "What is he/she trying to accomplish" is an important question. There have been a number of times when a family member presented a problem. I immediately went into my problem solving/ decision making formula. However, my wife or daughter didn't want advice. They simply wanted me to listen and understand what they were going through. I missed their purpose and responded inappropriately.

It's also important to understand your purpose. Why are you listening? Is it to build or strengthen a social relationship? Gain information and facts? Define a problem? The more you understand the speaker's and your own purpose, the higher the probability you will stay focused on the right things.

Hearing the words
Hearing is the physical component of listening. It requires functioning ears and a nervous system to transmit signals. An executive states, "Hearing the words is the first step of the listening process. Each word is important because one word can change the meaning of a message." Also, be aware of filtering the message. That occurs when people selectively listen to certain comments and screen out other statements. People may filter out the comments that don't agree with their point of view.

Hearing each word requires focus and concentration. Give the speaker your undivided attention. Eliminate distractions. Competing conversations, phones, radios, and other distractions can cause you to miss part of what's being said.

Internal distractions can also cause people to miss part of what's being said. Listening is hard work and one's attention can wander at times. Sometimes people concentrate more on what they will say back to the speaker. When your attention wanders, say focus words to yourself such as "tune-in" or "concentrate." These reminders help you stay in the present moment and listen.

Pay attention to the speaker's tone of voice and the words he or she emphasizes. Being "tone conscious" helps you pick up the subtle messages wrapped around the words.

Determine what is the most important part of the message —the facts and details or the main ideas. For example, if your boss is scheduling a meeting, the details of time, place and purpose may be most important. On the other hand, if the president of the company is giving a "state of the business" presentation, key ideas are most important. If needed, take notes to capture the important information.

Observing body language
What people say is important. How they deliver the message is equally important. The "words" of a message tell us what a person is thinking. The speaker's "body language" provides insight into what the person is feeling. Experts estimate that 50% to 70% of the message is interpreted through the nonverbal information that is conveyed.

Square and face the speaker. Make eye contact. Observe things like the following: gestures, speed of movement, and facial expressions including smiles, frowns, blinks and yawns. What can the nonverbal signals tell you about the speaker? They provide additional clues about what is really being said.

However, analysis of body language is subjective. Don't jump to conclusions at the first sight of a frown or yawn. Look for **patterns** in non-verbal behavior.

Interrelationships
The three parts of listening triangle—understanding purpose, hearing the words and observing body language—are essential parts of the listening process. Effective listeners also ask appropriate questions to clarify or gain additional information about each part of the listening triangle.

- "What's your objective in this meeting?"
- "Could you repeat the last part of what you just said?"
- "What do you mean by poor morale?"

A CEO of a major corporation is fond of saying, "Better questions produce better results." Effective communicators know that the right question will help the speaker provide the details or examples needed to clarify the message. An executive said, "If you're not in sync with the speaker, ask questions. Get the missing information. Also, don't be afraid of long pauses. Silence can lead the speaker to divulge more information."

Listening also involves analysis. Dissecting the message. Breaking the whole into its parts and seeing how the parts fit together to make the whole. Analysis often includes reflecting on these types of questions:

- Is the speaker presenting facts or opinions?
- Where did the data come from?
- What logic is the speaker using?
- What examples is the speaker using to support his views?
- What conclusions are being made?
- How does the message square with your beliefs and values?

Proper analysis helps you figure out what questions to ask or how to respond to the speaker.

Communication is a difficult process whether you are the sender or receiver. When you throw a baseball or football, you can watch and see if it's caught. When ideas are thrown back and forth, it's often difficult to know what's understood. The best listeners periodically validate their interpretation of the message. Comments like, "My understanding of your point is…" or "I interpret you to be saying…" are used as lead-ins to paraphrase the speaker's key ideas. If you are off the mark, it gives the speaker a chance to immediately correct the misunderstanding. Proper paraphrasing builds rapport and strengthens relationships.

Summary
Jerry Pepper, associate professor, University of Minnesota Duluth says that if you ask students what makes a good advisor, ask patients what makes a good doctor, ask employees what makes a good manager, the answers will include people who listen before judging, listen before directing, and listen before lecturing. The common theme—they listen first, then respond.

Being a good listener is hard work. It starts with being curious and having a real interest in people's ideas. Bottom line—effective listening helps you acquire new ideas and strengthen relationships.

In addition, it prevents problems, which saves time, effort and money.

Applying the Concept

Jan Morton, President, Self-Us-Team Collaborative

My clients include small business owners as well as managers and leaders from small and large companies. Basically, I'm hired to help an individual or a team be more effective—improve their performance. Improvement means change. The first thing I try to do is determine the level of receptivity. Is the person/team open to change or is there resistance? The client's body language gives me clues as to what's going on which is sometimes different from what they are telling me. There is a difference between "content" and "intent." The words mean one thing, sometimes the inflection or body language tells a different story.

I use a lot of mirroring or paraphrasing of what I'm hearing. I frequently use comments like, "Help me understand your comment about..." I often press for specifics. When I paraphrase, I synthesize the content and the intent. I try hard to capture both their words and their deeper meaning. I've also learned it's important to ask questions in a way that doesn't appear I'm looking for a certain answer.

Total focus and concentration on listening is hard work. Being a good listener has helped me understand my clients' real needs and their readiness to change. The big payoff is increased rapport with the client, deeper understanding of what's really going on, and a greater likelihood that what I do will make a positive difference.

Chapter 6
The Power Triangle

Parents, teachers, coaches, managers and leaders have power. Coaches decide who plays and who sits on the bench. Teachers assign homework, give tests and submit final grades. Leaders energize people to pursue bigger ideas and bigger goals. A colleague states, "With power you get people to do things even when they don't want to. Real leaders use their power in a positive way. Their focus is on the needs of people and their organization."

Power is derived from three sources:

- Position in the organization
- Personal characteristics
- Expertise

Position Power
Position power results from the manager's position in the organization. The chain of command gives managers power over the people below. Managers have the power to set goals, schedule meetings, assign work, and evaluate performance.

THE TRIANGLES OF MANAGEMENT AND LEADERSHIP

How much power does a manager have? Paul Hersey and Ken Blanchard, authors of *Management of Organizational Behavior*, make the point that the amount of power you're given depends on the level of trust and confidence your boss has in you. For example, a manager may be given more or less authority than his peers or his predecessor. In my opinion, authority is 70% given and 30% taken. Aggressive managers don't ask permission. They take action and then ask for forgiveness if needed.

One aspect of position power is having the authority to reward people. Managers can dole out desirable things such as praise, recognition, pay raises, promotions, shift assignments, special projects and opportunities to attend seminars. Effective use of rewards and recognition can motivate people to exceed expectations. People who use this type of power are very comfortable at center stage giving out awards and plaques. These events receive lots of publicity. For example, pictures of these ceremonies are often included in the company newspaper.

Position power also gives managers the power to force people to complete specific tasks or suffer the consequences. A manager states, "When I use coercive power, I force people to comply. They know I'm not afraid to hold people accountable and deliver negative consequences." Managers can withhold pay raises, administer discipline, and assign unpleasant tasks. However, overuse of coercive power creates an environment of fear. Can you control people through fear? The answer is a qualified "yes." You can control people's behavior but not their passion and enthusiasm. Phil Beaudoin, leadership consultant, remarks, "If you simply want people to obey the rules a bit of fear is good. On the other hand, if you want creativity and innovation get rid of the fear."

Through position power, managers also control resources such as information, budgets, and a network of contacts. Information is power. Managers can decide how much information to share and with whom. Also, managers can utilize their network of contacts to help others make the connections needed for success.

Position power gives you authority to reward and punish people, allocate resources and help people make the right connections.

Personal Power
As the name implies, this power derives from the leader's personal qualities. Personal power is often called charisma. Leaders such as Jack Welch, Tom Peters, and Mary Kay have tremendous charisma. Management consultant John Nicoletta asserts, "They make a gut-level connection with people. They engage people. Charismatic leaders are among the best at selling their ideas."

People with strong personal power have many of the following characteristics:

- They have lots of energy and enthusiasm for what they want to achieve (their vision) and how to achieve it (their strategies). Their enthusiasm is contagious. It gets others excited about what's possible.
- They are very self-confident. They're 100% convinced that they know what needs to be done. Doubts and waffling don't exist.
- Self-promotion is a common trait. They believe in themselves and aren't shy about marketing their talents and successes.
- They affirm people. They express confidence in people's ability to succeed.
- They have big personalities.

People with charisma are optimistic. They see the glass as overflowing with possibilities. Their focus is on the upside of any opportunity. They downplay the problems and potential risks. Charismatic leaders have the power to convince people that they can overcome the obstacles and achieve their goals.

Expert Power
Dr. W. Edwards Deming was an expert on quality and implementing quality systems. Experts have intimate knowledge in a particular field or discipline. They know what to do and how to do it. They're always up-to-date and current in their field. Experts simplify the complex. They frame the issue and provide clear and efficient shortcuts to decision-making.

An executive stated, "Being recognized as the 'best' at something is often crucial to having expertise power." For example, if you are known as the best at negotiating contracts, designing cars or selling computers, you have expertise power. The ideas and opinions of the expert are highly valued. Excellence and expertise demand people's attention. However, people with expertise must be willing to step forward and present their ideas.

Early in my career I worked in the Human Resources Department at the Hamilton Standard Division of United Technologies. Every six to twelve months I moved into a new area to learn about training, recruiting, compensation, benefits, and labor relations. One of my colleagues gave me the following advice: "It's great to have a broad understanding of all aspects of HR. But you also need to become an expert in at least one area. Experts have a depth of knowledge. They have dissected their subject down to its most basic atoms and molecules. They see the parts and how the parts connect to make the whole. That level of understanding will help you understand the dynamics in other areas."

Interrelationships

Each type of power tends to affect the other power bases. For example, people who have expertise and personal skills get noticed. They're often selected for management positions, thus gaining position power. As managers' position power increases, their network expands. This provides opportunities to benchmark, share ideas, discuss business trends, and learn new skills. Interacting with a large network of people broadens your frame of reference and understanding of what it takes to succeed.

Losing Power

One way to lose power is to never use it. "In 12 years, he has never praised or recognized any of his employees." Another way to lose power is to threaten poor performers but never deliver the punishment—"tough talk but no consequence." Experts can lose power by not keeping up to date in their area of expertise. People quickly lose credibility if they are viewed as being behind the times. Also, experts can lose their power if they become invisible. If they never demonstrate their expertise do they really have it?

Summary

Power—if you don't have any, you're not going to get much done. The more sources of power you have, the greater your chance of making an impact. Effective leaders aren't afraid to use their position, expertise and personal skills to challenge and stretch people to achieve organizational goals.

Applying the Concept

Steven Keeva, Author and Legal Journalist

I haven't sought power just to have it. My motivation is to help people achieve their goals. "Power" is a means to an end. To the extent that I have power, I've acquired it by becoming an expert in my field. My focus is finding deeper meaning and greater fulfillment in the practice of law. Because of this expertise people come to me asking for advice and guidance, and sometimes ask me to speak to various audiences.

It seems to me one way to acquire power is to find something that interests you deeply, preferably something that is new and fresh. Take steps to learn all you can, and try to put your own spin on the subject. It's also very important to keep up-to-date in your area of expertise. If you concentrate on something that really interests you, that's easy to do.

Applying the Concept

Ira Chaleff, Executive Coach and Author, *The Courageous Follower: Standing up to and For Our Leaders*

There is an obvious power differential between individuals in different positions of authority within an organization. Expertise can close some, and sometimes all of the gap. But, regardless of your relative lack of positional power or expert power, there is one personal characteristic that can even the playing field.

Aristotle asserted that of all the virtues, courage is the most essential as it activates the other virtues. What good is intelligence if you are afraid to speak your mind to an intimidating CEO? What good is compassion if you are afraid to intervene when colleagues are mistreating a minority employee? To be effective, courage must be accompanied by other virtues such as prudence, skill, commitment and honesty. But these without courage are greatly minimized.

I have always gravitated towards leadership positions. But, in most cases, I still reported to other leaders with more positional power than I had. History proved that when I spoke up to a more senior leader, confronting him or her about a counterproductive policy or behavior, our relationship grew stronger. When I was too timid to take a stand on issues I should have, the leader and the organization got itself into trouble that hurt everyone involved.

Now, as an executive coach, I find the same dynamics operating. It is always better for my effectiveness and my relationship with my clients if I tell them the truth about how I am experiencing their behavior, as long as I do so supportively. I've yet to be fired for doing this.

My advice to managers who want to acquire more power is this:

- *Make sure that your motivation for wanting power is to advance the legitimate mission of the group.*
- *Don't crave power so much that you are unwilling to lose it by speaking truth as you see it to those who have more power.*
- *Always work to improve your technical and interpersonal skills and your self-knowledge so that you are a worthy steward of power.*

THE TRIANGLES OF MANAGEMENT AND LEADERSHIP

- *Remember that whatever force created life gave us both free will and the capacity for power—make choices that use the power you acquire to serve life well.*

Chapter 7
Managing the Process

Managers manage processes. A process is a series of steps involving some combination of materials, equipment, information and people. Processes produce products and services.

Products are tangible things like books, bikes and baked goods. Customers evaluate products by various criteria including appearance, functionality, features, and price, taste and smell.

Services, on the other hand, aren't tangible. They involve the interaction between the customer and service provider. A marriage counselor interacts with a client by asking questions, discussing ideas and concepts. There is no tangible product. You can't put a service in inventory or resell it like you can a product.

At a restaurant, service includes things like the interaction between customer and wait staff, as well as how long it takes to be seated and served. I evaluate service by the wait staff's attitude, friendliness, listening skills and knowledge of the menu.

To describe a process, take a verb like interview, add "ing" and follow it with a direct object. You have defined a process. Some examples:

THE TRIANGLES OF MANAGEMENT AND LEADERSHIP

- Interviewing candidates
- Paying bills
- Assembling parts
- Counseling clients
- Resolving customer complaints

Effective organizations have clearly defined, efficient processes that produce quality products and services.

There are three parts to a process—inputs, process steps and output. Managers have to understand the critical elements in each of these areas.

Inputs
Inputs are the requests for products and services that come from both within and outside the organization. Examples include:

- External customers—"I'd like to order the shrimp dinner."
- Internal customers—A manager says to the human resources director, "I want to hire six software engineers."
- Boss—"Assemble 28 MX units by the end of the quarter."
- Team leader—"Our task is to establish a marketing plan by the end of the month."

Inputs must be specific and clearly defined. Quantity, quality standards, and due dates must be nailed down. Sometimes the input is a problem statement. A former CIO for a large financial services company states, "We would often get input from functional groups that were vague problems. They had a problem and they wanted us to solve it. We had to do a lot of questioning and probing to frame the real need. You can waste a lot of time if you simply react to every request you receive."

Bottom line—if the input isn't clear, there's a high probability that the output will not meet the customers' expectations.

The Process

The process includes the resources and the steps required to produce an output. For example, the process of baking a cake includes:

1. Obtain ingredients including cake mix, three eggs, water, oil and flour.
2. Preheat oven to 350°F.
3. Grease pans and dust with flour.
4. Blend in large bowl at low speed: cake mix, 3 egg whites, 1cup water and ¼ cup oil.
5. Beat 2 minutes at high speed.
6. Pour batter into pan.
7. Bake at 350°F for 40 minutes.
8. Cool cake in pan for 10 to 20 minutes.
9. Remove from pan.

In a similar way, any work process can be broken down into its major steps. A flowchart is a written description of all the steps, actions, and decisions made in a work process. Flowcharting helps you understand what's really going on from start to finish. Tony Borgen, expert in quality systems, asserts, " It's important to know the steps, people, decision making, handoffs and the measures used in a process."

Very often one of the process steps involves obtaining materials or information from suppliers. It's important to understand who your suppliers are and the quality of the material or information they provide. The old axiom "garbage in, garbage out" still applies.

Are the process steps known, understood and followed? Some important questions to consider include:

- Are the process steps written down?
- How does a new employee know what to do?

The amount of variation in the process will determine the amount of variation in the output. For example, if I use different ingredients or follow different steps each time I bake a cake, my output will vary significantly. The emphasis on quality is all about reducing variation. Consistency is important. However, some companies are consistently lousy. Your goal is to consistently produce products and services that meet and often exceed customer expectations.

The Output
The output is the completed product or service—baked cake, paid bill, assembled unit or completed counseling session.

Improving the Process
Competitive pressure requires you to constantly improve your process. Companies that have a "business as usual" culture don't last very long. Ongoing feedback from customers is important. What do they like? Dislike? How easy is it for the customer to use the output? Many times a customer will say "service was fine …but," or "quality is good…but." Don't stop listening after hearing the good stuff. When the customer says "fine…but," that's the time to listen aggressively and ask probing questions.

Can the process steps be simplified? A management consultant claims that whenever he looks at a business process he can always find waste. Waste is anything that is unnecessary or doesn't add value. It's important to eliminate waste, fight clutter and constantly simplify your process.

Benchmark the best. Observe and study what the best companies do. Beg, borrow, and try out new ideas to improve your process. Carla O'Dell says that benchmarking starts by having the right attitude. You must be humble enough to admit that someone else is better at something, and wise enough to learn from them.

Summary
Michael Hammer, author and guru on process management, believes that effective and efficient processes are even more critical today than they were 10 years ago. There are always opportunities to improve your processes and "wow" customers. Hammer maintains we don't need heroes (employees who go the extra mile to satisfy the customer). We just need great processes.

Applying the Concept

Michael Keleher, Author and Consultant

Customer satisfaction means I'm producing consistent products and services, which my customers value. The purpose of process management is to create predictability. "A good cake every time," as it were. Process management for me is useful in eliminating repetitive tasks. Whatever the project—writing an article, developing a product promotion, or consulting, there is a series of steps I must follow. By having a step-by-step framework I know what has to be done. A key lesson I've learned is that the most efficient process in the world is worthless if the inputs (what the customer wants) aren't clear. Sometimes inputs can be incomplete, incorrect or just fluid. In cases like these, when I start a project I check in with the customer early and often to make sure we're on the same page. Sometimes I have to adapt my process or create a new one to be responsive to the customer.

Applying the Concept

Eric Schneider, Quality Engineer, Birken Manufacturing Company

As a quality engineer, I use process management to understand and offer improvements for everything from order entry at the front end of the business, through manufacturing and shipping. Whether it's in the office or manufacturing plant, the tools of "process management" are the same.

I find it's best to start by flowcharting the process. A graphic flow chart with lines and arrows tells me much more than reading a "text only" procedure. Written text can be dull. A flowchart gives me a picture of what's happening. It also tells me if "rework" is being done to correct mistakes that happened earlier in the process. Another important aspect of process management is making it clear what's being measured. People are motivated to use the process management tools because they see positive changes in the metrics or measures.

Process management is a simple concept that "wows" the customer when they experience improvements in products and services.

Chapter 8
The Three Phases of Planning

Having a vision and communicating it to your organization is important. Equally important is having appropriate plans in place to take you to the promised land.

Planning has three parts:

- Goal setting
- Development of plans
- Implementation

I've found some people have goals but no plan. "I want to make a million dollars but don't know how I'm going to do it." Others have goals and a plan but never take action to implement their plan. "Joe's all talk, no action." Needless to say, all three activities—setting goals, developing plans and implementing the plans—are important for individual and organizational success.

Goal Setting
One of Stephen Covey's seven habits of effective people is "to begin with the end in mind." That's good advice for goal setting. What do you want to achieve? What's the deliverable?

How should goals be established? As discussed in chapter 3, managers can use a directing, discussing, or delegating style. A company president might simply announce, "Our strategic goals are the following..." A manager working with his employee may spend 30 minutes discussing what needs to be accomplished over the next 12 months. Using a delegating style I might say to an employee, "I want you to identify your top five to seven goals for the next 12 months." In general, the more involved employees are in setting goals, the more motivated they will be to achieve them.

Strategic goals are usually longer term and are focused on the total organization. "Our goal is to increase market share from 20% to 30%." Once goals are established it's important to prioritize them. Most organizations establish five to eight strategic goals. Only a limited number of goals can be pursued at any one time. Having too many goals is as bad as having no goals.

Departments, teams and individuals must establish short and long term goals that support the strategic goals.

Effective goals meet the following criteria:

- Specific—Pinpoint what you want. Vague goals like "improve quality" or "cut costs" are open to wide interpretations and can't be measured.
- Appropriate—Goals must be set within the context of what's going on in the marketplace. An 8% cost reduction may just keep you in the game. A 15% reduction may be needed to lead the pack.
- Time-bounded—Specific dates and times provide focus and reduce confusion. Goals without deadlines have a way of slipping away.

Leaders and managers need to be able to effectively explain <u>why</u> the stated goals are important. Employees want to know why, for example, they have to increase their productivity by 30%. I've found it's best to explain needed improvements in terms of what's going on in the marketplace. Competition is real. Most people understand the need to meet or exceed what the competition is doing.

The Plan
The plan answers the question, "How are we going to achieve the goal?" Let's say my goal is to get from Boston to New York City. I have many options. I can fly, take a train, bus, drive, jog, walk or even crawl.

A strategic plan also answers the question, "How will we compete in the marketplace?" Why will customers buy your products and services? A variety of approaches are used to establish a competitive advantage, including offering a large selection, low prices, great quality, and the latest technology. Dr. Fred Wiersema, author of *The Discipline of Market Leaders,* recommends doing one thing better than anybody in the industry. For example, Walmart is the best at offering low prices. The senior management team of Walmart has to establish a plan as to how they will offer the lowest prices and still achieve their profit goals. The management team has to determine what organizational structure, processes, systems, and vendor arrangements will be needed to achieve the lowest cost. All the organizational pieces must be aligned and support the company's strategic competitive advantage.

Overall plans break down into work processes, projects, and at the most basic level, tasks. Chapter 4 discusses work processes.

Projects are major initiatives taken to achieve departmental and organizational goals. A work breakdown structure identifies all the tasks in a project. It's best to list all tasks as action items, such as

- Define hardware requirements
- Interview candidates
- Conduct design review

It's also important to define who is responsible for each task.

A plan is a roadmap to accomplish a goal. It describes the specific steps and actions required to go from point A to point B. Plans will vary in the amount of structure and detail at each level in the organization.

Contingency plans should be developed to cope with favorable as well as adverse changes. Having the ability to react quickly to changing circumstances is important.

Implementation

Mead Corporation has a 600 pound rock in their lobby. Steve Mason, Mead's CEO, says that the rock is a metaphor to remind people what it takes to move the rock. Meetings and planning sessions to discuss how to move the rock may be useful. However, the rock doesn't move until someone implements the plan.

In an article, "The Smart-Talk Trap," authors Jeffrey Pfeffer and Robert Sutton make the point that in business there is a willingness to let talk substitute for action. And the smarter a person sounds the more likely talk may substitute for action. Some people emphasize the talking, analyzing, debating, dialoging, and discussing part of the equation at the expense of the "doing."

What separates the best companies from the average ones? Execution—flawless implementation of the plan. I've heard some coaches say, "I'll give the opponent our game plan. We win on execution."

What does it take to implement a plan?

- Assign responsibility. I'm a big believer in establishing single point accountability. Without focused accountability it's very easy for things to get confused and fall in a crack. "Everybody was sure somebody would do it but nobody did."
- Establish a deadline to begin and complete the project or task. A former managing director of Toyota states, "Without deadlines tasks are far less likely to be completed. Deadlines also help employees prioritize their work."
- Establish appropriate controls. Define what feedback is needed and how frequently.
- Express confidence in the individual or team.

The "to do" list is the most basic level of implementation. The "to do" list includes things like setting up meetings, returning phone calls, and analyzing data. One problem with "to do" lists is people often write down low priority items. It feels like you're accomplishing a great deal as you achieve these C-priority items. To guard against this practice keep your high priority goals visible. For example, a middle manager remarks, "I write my 'to do' list at the beginning of each day. My top three goals for the year are always written across the top of the page. It keeps me focused on the right things."

I attend lots of meetings where participants go on at length about how their ideas will solve various problems. You can have the best ideas in the world but customers and senior management value people who turn ideas into action and results. No successful person has been described as long on philosophy and short on implementation.

Summary
Effective managers know that all three variables—focused goals, complete plans, and flawless implementation—are required for success.

Applying the Concept

Sharon Gazda, President, Edizen

In managing my own business, I first set financial goals because my planning spins off from there. Once I have established a financial goal, I break the revenues into quarters, then I break the numbers by month. By understanding how many billable days I should be working, I can plan how many projects to undertake.

I think this is a fairly standard method for those of us who "sell" services. I have met many exceptional professionals who fail at consulting because they do not consider the sales side of the business.

My advice for new managers is to decide what matters most and stick to it. It took Ford and General Motors a few bleak years before they realized that "Quality is Job One." Repeat your goals often, post them around the office, and find fun ways to reinforce them at every opportunity. Your employees should be able to recite without hesitation the top three goals of your department or division. Also, make sure your goals are aligned with the company's strategic objectives.

Set goals higher, and stretch the performance of your employees. That's better than setting low goals just so employees can meet them. People know when they are being challenged, and don't accept average performance. Employees respect those who challenge them.

Sometimes managers create task lists instead of goals. Goals are something you work toward, not something you do. Make sure you can measure all the verbs you use when you write goals. Words like re-evaluate, design, and improve can be very subjective. Every goal needs to be measurable.

Chapter 9
Decision Making

READY, AIM, FIRE!! Fast paced competition continues to shorten the length of time you're given to complete each action.

What decisions need to be made? Many decisions are insignificant, programmed, and routine, such as ordering parts and scheduling vacations. However, 10% of the decisions you make are major. They define who you are, where you're going, and what's important.

Decisions are made to solve problems and to create new opportunities. My focus is on problem solving. A problem exists when there is a gap between "what is happening" versus "what ought to be." Three important questions to ask when confronted with a problem: 1.Who owns the problem? (Just because you're presented with a problem doesn't mean you own it.) 2. How much time, effort, and money should go into solving the problem? (Not all problems are equal in importance.) 3. What approach should be used to address the problem? Should it be assigned to an individual? A team? Should an external consultant be hired?

Making a decision requires the following three actions:

- Define the problem
- Identify possible options
- Select the best option

Define the Problem
When asked how he would save the world in one hour, Albert Einstein said that he would spend 55 minutes defining the problem and the last five solving it. Managers can spend a lot of time solving the "wrong problem."

One of my mentors said, "Beware of people who have a solution before they understand the problem." Some managers have the attitude, "I've seen this problem before. I know the solution." Often the hardest part of problem solving is identifying the real problem. The presented problem may be a symptom of an underlying issue. Like Einstein, managers need to spend time making sure they pinpoint the "right" problem. Root cause analysis and asking "why" over and over are needed to peel back the onion.

What information do you need to define the problem? Data can be divided into two categories: "must have" and "nice to have." You'll never have the time and resources necessary to collect every piece of data. Focus on what's critical. As you collect data, it's important to separate facts from opinions, current status from past trends, and the points of view you're considering. For example, employees, customers and senior management may have very different views on how they see the problem.

How you ultimately define the problem is also important. I've heard people say, "The problem is we don't have enough computers." The obvious solution is "get more computers." A better problem statement might be "Work output is 18% less than what's required."

Many problems are complex and challenging. Often times there is not one expert who can simply state the problem. Multiple perspectives are needed. The issue needs to be discussed and analyzed before the real problem evolves. The motto "a problem well stated is half-solved" is time tested.

Identify Possible Options
"I have the solution, but it will cost a million dollars."

Identifying possible options must be done within a larger context. Points to consider include:

- How much time, effort, and money do you want to spend?
- Do you need a short-term fix or a long-term solution?
- What resources are currently available?
- What will the people who have to make it work accept?

Once the problem is clearly defined, usually one or more options will immediately come to mind. Force yourself to develop additional options. New ideas come from discovering new relationships. On a daily basis look for new ways to "connect the dots."

Brainstorm. Try to generate as many ideas as possible. Remove your "judgmental hat" and openly consider the unusual, different, off-the-wall ideas.

Be curious. Ask lots of questions. "How have other companies solved this problem?" "What would a 12-year old do?" Ayn LaPlant, President, Beekley Corporation, says, "I ask questions that focus people to find their own answers. The right question can also help people see an issue from a different angle. Asking questions that prod people to think differently can open up many new possibilities."

Benchmarking is another way to generate new ideas. LaPlant states, "I want our employees to look at other companies and find best practices. If you're really committed to continuous improvement, you have a natural curiosity to learn from the best."

Selecting the Best Alternative
Weigh all the facts and information. Apply good judgment, which is the ability to combine hard data, questionable data and intuitive guesses to select the best option.

Who should make the decision? It depends. Sometimes the leader knows best. Other times the team should make the decision.

How should the decision be made? I've heard people say, "I'm going with alternative A—the facts support it." "Well I like alternative B, call it a hunch." I think it's important to consider both the facts and your gut instinct.

Effective leaders and managers are decisive. They make timely decisions. Most people would prefer a "yes" or "no" decision to a long drawn out "maybe." Analysis paralysis, poor time management and ineffective meetings can often be traced back to an inability or unwillingness to make decisions.

Some people experience anxiety when making the smallest decision. Fear of failure and fear of success can keep individuals frozen, unable to move in any direction. Decisions spark action.

Summary
The decision-making triangle includes three interrelated steps. Each step is important. Joel Barker states, "Becoming a more efficient, more effective problem solver is one of the most powerful ways of shaping the world and achieving your vision."

Applying the Concept

Ed Corcoran, Senior Manager of Workers' Compensation Programs, Raytheon Corporation

Decision-making is not just for managers. All employees should be given responsibility for decision-making. I have invested significant time and effort into building an internal self-administered team that has been empowered to think and act creatively every day. A lot of the issues I deal with are problems that directly impact our "Risk and Claim Management" policies.

When problems arise, I start by visualizing where I want to be. What's my end goal? Next, I try to think about what has to change. Does the process need to change? Do people need training? Are the wrong people assigned the task? The third step—I try to determine what actions are necessary to make the change. On each step it's important to get good advice and guidance. I welcome diverse opinions.

Our company has implemented the Six Sigma concepts. In essence it means improving your process so you virtually don't make any mistakes. It's important to apply these concepts to the decision making process. I try to frequently ask myself questions like the following:

- Could the problem-solving/decision-making process have been more creative?
- Did I involve the "right" people?
- Did the decision lead to continued improvement in the organization?
- Are the decisions incorporating "best practices?"
- Is the approach I'm using encouraging and fostering teamwork?

All of the decisions people make determine the extent to which an organization achieves excellence.

Applying the Concept

Greg Thomas, President and founder of weLEAD Incorporated
www.leadingtoday.org

Decision-making is a necessity in our complex competitive business environment. Why is sound decision-making so vitally important? It is simply a matter of choice, and who gets to choose! I know that if I am unwilling to make a difficult decision, usually "time" will make the decision for me. I do not want to leave the success of my business to "time and chance" because I was unwilling to accept the risk of decision-making. It has been said the General Dwight Eisenhower once said, "a wrong decision is better than indecision." I believe this to be a sound principle. When I make a wrong decision I typically have the time to adjust or modify the original judgment to make it successful. Indecision only wastes precious time and often limits valuable options because of the delay.

Here are some of the things I do to encourage sound decision-making at weLEAD Inc.

1. *I set* deadlines *on projects and major decisions. Everyone in the organization should understand that a time limitation exists for the decision-making process of a project. Only during rare situations should the deadline be extended. These situations would include a sudden change in market or competitive environments that may legitimately be cause for reevaluation. If* potential *decisions are allowed to be openended without an established deadline, odds are that the tough decisions will be avoided!*

2. *Evaluate the* locus of control *of your entire management team. You may be in for a* shock *and it may provide an answer as to why some of your managers find it so hard to make difficult decisions. Your locus of control is a trait measured by a personality scale orginally developed by Julian Rotter. Most individuals have a tendency to have either a strong* internal *locus of control orientation or strong* external *locus of control orientation. Those with a strong* internal *locus of control believe most events that occur in their lives are determined by their* own actions *rather than by chance. In contrast, those with a strong* external *locus of control believe most events occur by chance or circumstance and conclude they have* little control *over fate, or to change their lives. Those with an* internal *orientation tend to accept more responsibility for their actions and for organizational performance. Research indicates they are also more flexible, innovative, adaptive*

and take more initiative in solving problems. What is your locus of control orientation? Perhaps some of your key management personnel have an orientatation toward an external locus of control! Once this is confirmed there are definite steps that can be taken to modify their behavior.

3. *What if you determine that <u>you</u> have a problem with decision-making? The answer is to compensate by getting help. Effective leaders acknowledge they have weaknesses and learn to rely on associates or peers who have the strengths they lack. Ask a few close associates to confidentially come to you and alert you of your tendency to avoid decisions when it becomes evident to them. Don't shoot the messenger, and use the alert to prod yourself into action. Part of the solution to this problem is recognizing the problem in yourself, or your team, and taking the necessary steps to modify and change behavior.*

Chapter 10
Three Approaches to Managing Conflict

Conflict exists when people are in disagreement.

Conflict is good! It shows people are passionate, committed, and willing to fight for their ideas. Conflict is bad! People stop listening and become more and more entrenched in their position. A senior manager asserts, "High levels of stress can produce more of the 'bad conflicts.' With dysfunctional conflict, people become aggressive and focus on winning and being right. When challenged, they become angry and defensive."

Karl Slaikeu, author, *Controlling the Cost of Conflict,* says that every organization has conflict. People are never going to see things exactly the same, nor should they. Conflict can occur with bosses, customers, suppliers, and peers.

Where do we disagree?
When conflict occurs, it's important to analyze and diagnose the areas where you disagree and potential reasons why you disagree. The disagreement can be over a number of things such as power, goals, priorities, plans, workload, time pressure and competition for scarce resources. I've heard people generalize and say, "We disagree on everything." That's usually not the case. Often a more

accurate description is, " We agree on the goals but disagree on the approach needed to get there."

Why do we disagree?
Conflicts can be caused by factors including different assumptions or needs, inaccurate or incomplete information, inarticulate communications, and poor listening skills. A manager states, "I frequently disagree with Collin. His frame of reference, his views about people are very different from mine." Our "mental model" or "frame of reference" causes us to view situations a certain way. These different points of view often lead to disagreements. A management consultant states, "It's important to learn as much as you can about the nature of the conflict. What are the stakes for the other party? How do they see the issue? What are their needs?"

There are three basic approaches to managing conflict:

- Compete
- Compromise
- Collaborate

Most people have a dominant conflict-resolution style. I think it's important to know when and how to use all three styles.

The following basic principles should be followed regardless of the conflict management approach you're using.

- Attack the issue, not the person.
- Listen with empathy. Try to fully understand the other person's viewpoint.
- Present your ideas clearly and forcefully.
- Disagree without being disagreeable.

Keep in mind that every conflict has two aspects—the issue at hand and the relationship between the parties. Each approach to managing conflict produces a different combination of win/lose results for the people involved.

Compete
Like participating in sports, when you compete you're trying to win. The compete approach is often used in labor-management disputes. Each party has opposing goals and interests. When using this approach, the perceptions of each group often become distorted. This approach produces a win/lose result.

In what situations should you compete?

- The disagreement involves a high priority consequence. You have expertise and are very committed to your position.
- There is not a major need to maintain a positive relationship with the other person.

How should you compete?
Present your case in a clear and compelling fashion. Use facts, data, and testimonials to support your position. Influential people have strong points of view. Their conviction and determination come across in how the message is delivered.

Attack the other person's proposal. Question their assumptions and logic. Create doubts that their approach will really work.

There is a time and place for win-lose competition. However, it's worth noting that the "loser" often goes away angry, plotting his approach to win the next round.

Compromise
"Half a loaf is better than no bread." Compromise is trying to reach a middle ground. Compromise can be used effectively when the goal sought can be divided equitably, such as money or time. If that isn't possible one party must give up something of value as a concession.

Compromise produces a win/lose result. Both parties get some of what they want but not all.

In what situations should you compromise?

- The disagreement involves the legitimate needs of both parties.
- Both parties are open and willing to move from their initial position.
- There is a need to maintain a positive relationship with the other person.

How should you compromise?
Many times people think a compromise must end up close to the middle. For example, if I'm selling my car for $10,000 and you offer $5,000, is the compromise price $7,500? Not necessarily. There are degrees of compromise. I might say my lowest price is $8,500. People move at different rates from their initial position.

Compromise is a traditional way to resolve conflicts. Compromise is based on negotiations, give and take. People who lack good negotiating skills can end up giving up more than they get.

Collaborate
Collaboration involves working together to solve problems and create new alternatives which are beneficial for both parties. It's based on trust. Building trust begins when one party is willing to

risk opening up and communicating exactly what he is thinking and feeling. The law of reciprocity says, "give what you want to receive." If one side opens up, there is a good chance the other side will follow. This approach is the only style that has a win/win orientation.

In what situations should you collaborate?

- There is trust and openness to share information.
- Both parties are motivated to search for creative solutions.

How should you collaborate?
Dissect the disagreement. Take the problem apart and closely examine each component. Be curious. Ask "why" and "what if" questions. "Why is this conflict occurring after the reorganization?" "What if we change our assumptions?"

Use brainstorming. This technique requires that any and all ideas are recorded in a non-judgmental setting. Critiquing ideas and selecting possible solutions is done later.

Developing creative solutions through collaboration often produces new and innovative ideas. In addition, it builds and strengthens the relationship between the parties.

Summary
Conflict is inevitable. However, efforts should be made to try and prevent unnecessary conflict. Different situations require different approaches to managing conflict. The effective management of conflict can produce positive change.

Applying the Concept

Stewart Levine, founder, Resolution Works, and author, *Getting to Resolution: Turning Conflict into Collaboration*

As a "recovering" lawyer I spent many years playing the litigation game. It's the mode of choice in many institutional settings. Unfortunately most people don't realize that as long as the competition continues, a transactional cost of staying in the conflict is paid. The knee jerk reaction most people have is to compete and try to win. It's part of our culture. We spend the third Sunday of every January wondering who will "win" and who will "lose." Unfortunately the cost of any conflict often negates any real winner.

Compromise is a step in the right direction. At least you stop paying the costs of being in the conflict. But it assumes the posture of distributive bargaining—we only have one pie to divide—the more for me, the less for you. The real goal is collaboration—sharing ideas and real concerns, using creativity to figure out how to take care of everyone's needs.

What can managers do when conflict occurs?

- *Recognize everyone within an organization is inside the same circle, on the same team. They have the same goals: pride in the product or service provided, satisfying relationships and financial rewards.*
- *Start off by asking, "What am I doing or not doing that is contributing to this conflict?"*
- *Accept that all conflict happens at the personality level. Once you can disengage from that emotional battle the solution is not difficult to find.*

- Listen and find out what people need, then use your creativity to figure out how to give it to them.
- When others come to you with a conflict to resolve: 1. Send them away to solve it themselves; 2. If they come back again, act as a facilitator; 3. Make the decision

Applying the Concept

John Nicoletta, Managing Partner, Be the Leader Associates

In 1966, I was a 21-year-old college student. The times were turbulent and political debate was heated. I held some strong beliefs, and being a senior, I knew I was "right."

One of my classmates was a 25-year military veteran. For four years we crossed paths and often engaged in strong disagreements on a broad array of issues. These disagreements were often played out as classroom debates. We had come to develop a genuine mutual dislike for each other and our disagreements had become more heated.

One day a political debate developed between several students in the cafeteria. Ultimately it came down to a nose to nose confrontation between me and my 25-year military "friend." There was a large audience and at some point I believe I made the decision to enter into a win/lose approach and cause my classmate to be discredited and lose face.

He eventually lost his temper and had to be restrained by several onlookers as he tried to physically attack me. At the time, I considered this a complete victory. The intellectual matching of wits was relegated to a physical confrontation. From that day on, we avoided each other and never had another confrontation.

On reflection, it now seems to me that I made a conscious decision to take on a win/lose strategy to deal with conflict. I believe that a win/lose strategy is only acceptable when three conditions are met:
1. *When the need to win is high.*
2. *When the need to maintain the relationship is low.*
3. *When you have the authority to impose the victory.*

I think, at the time, I would have said that those conditions were met in my conflict with my classmate.

First: The need to win was high and loss was unacceptable. In this situation I was convinced of the righteousness of my position. This was a clash between right thinking versus wrong thinking. I had to win. Condition met.

Second: The need to maintain the relationship was low. I was convinced that I would never "break bread" nor "cross paths" with my classmate after we left school. Condition met.

Third: Did I have the authority to make my position prevail? Yes. I clearly was representing the "moral high ground." Right wins over might. Condition met.

Ten years later I was desperately trying to re-enter the teaching profession. Jobs were scarce. I had finally interviewed for the "perfect" position. Every hurdle had been cleared. This school practiced team teaching. The final step was a meeting with the other team members to gain their approval. It was in the bag.

When I entered the room to meet my future team members, my heart sank when I saw sitting and smiling broadly at me my "old friend" from college. He was gracious and friendly. Needless to say I did not get the job.

When you think that a win/lose strategy for dealing with conflict is called for and that all the conditions have been met to justify this approach, think again. Go back and double check. Think it through carefully. Is it really impossible to find a win/win solution?

Chapter 11
The ABCs of Motivation

Business, like sports, is very competitive. Customers want better quality and lower prices. Stockholders want more profit and bigger dividends. The competition continues to expand and improve. Winning in sports and business requires top performance.

What motivates people to consistently perform at their best? What can managers do to motivate their employees? Practice the ABCs of motivation. "A" stands for *antecedents*, "B" for *behavior* and "C" for *consequences.*

Antecedents
Antecedents are the things managers and leaders say or do that cause employee behavior to occur. Examples of antecedents include:

- Assigning tasks—"*Interview 15 customers and identify their top three complaints.*"
- Describing the importance of the work—"*This project is critical to our long term success.*"
- Setting goals—"*Sell three new cars per month.*"
- Establish deadlines—"*Complete this project by 10:00 a.m Friday.*"

- Describe incentives—*"If you complete this project on time and within budget, you'll receive a $500.00 bonus."*
- Explain penalties for non-performance— *"If you don't deliver the desired results, you're fired."*
- Affirm the individual— *"You have great talents in..."*
- Ask questions—*"What do you think we should do?"*
- Point out top performance—*"Watch Maureen. She's outstanding at handling customer complaints."*

Managers often use a combination of antecedents when interacting with employees. What's said or not said to employees can influence their motivation.

How the antecedent is delivered is also important. The delivery can run the gamut from polite and professional to threating and screaming. The "how-it's-delivered" part of the equation may have more impact than <u>what</u> is said. For example, I recently observed the following:

A father said to his 8-year-old daughter, "It's time to put your toys away and go to bed." The child kept playing. Five minutes later, the parent repeated the command. The child kept playing with her toys. For a third time, the father delivered the same message, but this time had a different tone of voice. The child responded. Toys were quickly put away. She said "goodnight" and went to bed. In this case the tone of voice triggered a reaction. Perhaps the child had learned that an unpleasant consequence would occur if behavior didn't change.

The question for managers and leaders is—What type of antecedent will yield the most positive reaction in the employee? And how should it be delivered? In general the right antecedent helps satisfy a person's strongest needs. For example, people who have a strong need for self-esteem like to be affirmed and feel valued. People who have a high achievement need want to know things such as, What has to be accomplished? What are the deadlines? And, how will quality be measured?

Leaders deliver their antecedent message with decisiveness, conviction, and enthusiasm. Leaders don't waffle. They don't project doubt or uncertainties when they speak. In addition, they have passion for their beliefs and initiatives.

People are unique. You need to determine which antecedents will motivate each of your employees.

Behavior
"B" stands for behavior. In this case it's what employees say or do following the antecedent. Their behavior is observable.

An important question is—"What behavior is desired?" One of my colleagues worked with a vice president of marketing who wanted to improve the performance of his organization. The VP said, "I want to have an outstanding sales force." When asked, "What does outstanding look like? What separates good from great performance?" the VP had no answers.

Managers also have to make sure one desired behavior doesn't negatively impact another desired behavior. One company in Arizona announced the following new policy, "If you're late for meetings you pay a $2.00 fine." The announcement of the policy was the antecedent. The desired behavior was being on time for meetings. People began to show up on time. However, in some cases people abruptly ended important phone calls with customers to be on time for a meeting.

Consequences

"C" stands for consequences. What managers say or do after an employee has completed a task is the consequence. The "right" consequence promotes continued positive behavior. Some examples of possible consequences include:

- Feedback—*"My observations are the following..."*
- Recognition/praise of the individual— *"You're very talented."*
- Recognition/praise for the work done-- *"The marketing plan is perfect."*
- Rewards—*"I'm giving you a $2,800 raise."*
- Increased power— *"I'm putting you in charge of the Alpha project."*
- Discipline/punishment— *"I'm giving you a verbal warning for ..."*
- Redo the work— *"This is unacceptable. Redo the report."*
- Coaching/training— *"Let me make two suggestions on..."*

I once heard a management consultant say, "The most common response to good or improved behavior is no response. It goes unnoticed." That's sad. Most people (not all) want to be noticed and to feel appreciated when their performance improves.

As stated with antecedents, how the consequence is delivered is important. The manager's attitude, tone of voice, and gestures send important signals about good and bad performance. In addition, who delivers the consequence can be significant. For example, feedback from a customer or team member may have more influence than feedback from the boss. That's why multi-rater, or 360 feedback (comments on performance from customers, peers, subordinates and bosses) is powerful.

Not all consequences produce the same results. Time off, choice assignments, feedback, discipline, increased power, small gifts, promotions and public recognition effect people in different ways. People's desires, needs, and openness to change do vary. For example, my daughter Kate hates to receive public recognition. My wife Mary Jean, on the other hand, loves it.

The timing of the consequence is also important. Generally the sooner the consequence is delivered, the more it will influence future behavior. Managers who wait for the annual performance appraisal to let people know how great or bad a job they're doing miss the boat.

Theories of reinforcement recommend continuous reinforcement to change a behavior. That is, every time the person displays the desired behavior, reward it. Punish undesired behavior. Once the new behavior has taken hold, use intermittent reinforcement. Provide positive consequences every once in a while

The consistency of the consequences can affect motivation. Employees often get unmotivated when they feel they are being unfairly treated. "John and I worked 26 hours of free overtime to complete the project. He received a day off; I received nothing." That's not fair. In cases like this people often adjust their contribution to match the reward level.

Summary
Having a highly motivated workforce is critical to compete in today's marketplace. All three variables—antecedents, desired behavior, and consequences—are important factors in the motivation equation. The right antecedents and consequences help employees achieve top performance.

How can managers discover the best antecedent/consequence for their employees? Ask people, "What motivates you?" Most people will readily tell you what they like and dislike. Pay attention to what's important to the person. As Will Rodgers said, "When you go fishing, you bait the hook not with what you like, but with what the fish likes."

Applying the Concept

Bart Slottje, Consultant, Quo Group Netherlands, and Editor of p-management.com

Last year I did some work at an international manufacturing company. The personnel manager, a supervisor and me, as an external consultant, were assigned the task of lowering absenteeism.

We did an ABC analysis of attendance and absenteeism to pinpoint both the undesirable and desirable behavior. We wanted to know what set the stage for the behavior to occur (antecedents) and what happened to the performer as a result of the behavior (consequences). Knowing this can help you make appropriate changes to achieve the desired behavior. We came up with the following list of employee beliefs and attitudes:
Antecedents: no feedback for coming in late or being absent; during the first 30 minutes nobody works anyway; we don't know what is expected from us; and performance appraisal has quality, not attendance as key result factor.
Consequences: can stay in bed longer; fewer traffic jams; no comments from the manager about being late; co-workers laugh about it; and you can still get a good appraisal.

The consequences supporting the undesirable behavior are positive for the employees and therefore increase the occurrence of the behavior in the future. An ABC analysis of the desirable behavior, a higher attendance, showed us few consequences supporting the desirable behavior. Our next step was to chance the consequences and the antecedents.

Consequences
One consequence we instituted was group feedback. A large graph showed how well a department was performing regarding attendance. The graph gave employees an opportunity to discuss attendance and the supervisor an opportunity to positively reinforce employees. Small rewards like coffee and donuts were used to reward improvements in attendance. Another consequence was that employees with perfect attendance had the opportunity to win prizes such as televisions and CD players. Each quarter a lottery was held to award prizes. On an annual basis employees were eligible to receive a monetary bonus of $250 if they had been absent three days or less.

Antecedents
Because the ABC analysis indicated employees didn't know what was expected of them, a guide was developed and distributed explaining the importance of attendance. In addition, absenteeism was made an important issue during appraisal interviews.

These changes in the antecedents and consequences had a positive effect on attendance. The director of the company said, "This resulted in not only better attendance, but also a boost in quality and productivity. Our position in the world market is stronger."

Applying the Concept

Tim Still, Vice President, Annuity Services, The Travelers

Managers should remember that they don't accomplish objectives, their direct reports do. I have eight managers reporting to me. My goal is to provide the right stimulus or antecedents and consequences to consistently bring out their best performance. Before applying the antecedent, you need to know the desired behavior.

<u>Antecedents</u>. I provide several types of antecedents with my direct reports. At the macro level, I discuss my philosophies. For example, I've spent a lot of time discussing process management, streamlining work, eliminating service backlogs, and rework being done by the person who caused it. I try to capture a lot of my philosophies in a phrase, such as "compensation equals contribution." People are more likely to remember a phrase. At the next level of detail, my managers and I establish goals for the month, quarter, and year. At the most specific level, I try to provide each manager with incentives that will motivate him/her. Each person has some unique needs. Some people respond to words of encouragement; others might be more motivated when given highly visible assignments and opportunities to present their work to senior management.

<u>Behavior</u>. I want my managers to follow and implement my philosophies. But I also want them to develop their own styles of managing. I want them to take responsibility for their own performance and results, and that of their respective teams.

Consequences. Customer feedback is a powerful consequence. I make sure the "voice of the customer" is heard frequently. When customers are happy, my managers and employees feel proud and satisfied. Other types of consequences for meeting or exceeding expectations include quarterly bonuses for meeting predefined measures for productivity and quality, pay increases for merit, pictures on the bulletin board, and words of praise for outstanding achievements in servicing the customer. If people aren't getting the job done the consequence is candid feedback. However, I've learned not to overreact to one event. Look at the performance trend. That's a better indicator.

The bottom line is that to motivate people, or help change their behavior, I have to change the As and Cs. The "right" antecedent and consequence get people's attention.

Chapter 12
The Art of Giving Feedback

Feedback is the mechanism that helps people discover the ideas, insights and information needed to increase their effectiveness. Without feedback it's "business as usual."

Can any of your employees validly make one of the following statements?

- My manager seldom lets me know how I'm doing.
- When I make a mistake, my boss attacks me.
- My manager always lets me know when I mess up but never lets me know how to improve.

Effective managers provide frequent and effective performance feedback.

Before giving feedback it's important to spend time observing and analyzing current performance. The following questions need to be answered. What's the person's understanding of his role? What's the quality and quantity of his work? What are his top priorities? What knowledge and skills does the person possess? What's his level of motivation? What is the person doing or not doing that negatively impacts performance?

Delivering effective feedback requires the following:

- A desire to help people improve
- A message that's clear and focused
- Appropriate timing for the delivery

Desire
It's easy to talk about a person's good traits and successes. However, many managers shy away from discussing an employee's poor performance. Author and management consultant Morris Shechtman says that many managers aren't candid and direct when giving performance feedback. Rather, they tell people what they want to hear, and then complain when people don't change. For example, a manager in one of my leadership seminars admitted he didn't want to confront his secretary's poor job performance. He felt negative feedback would upset her and cause her to do even less work.

How can managers expect continuous improvement if they don't provide candid feedback? When managers don't confront poor job performance, employees conclude, "I'm meeting expectations. I'm performing at an acceptable level." One senior manager states, "It takes desire and courage to confront people. You can't worry about people being upset or angry with you. Your focus needs to be on helping people be the best they can be."

Giving feedback starts with desire and willingness to help people achieve their best performance. Without desire, managers say nothing and stand by watching people "underperform."

The Message

How you package the message is important. Most people don't like to hear about their weaknesses. However, they are usually open to suggestions about how to be more effective. Your message must be clear, succinct and organized.

Start by explaining the purpose of the meeting. "We're here to discuss the ..." Ask the person to listen carefully to all of your comments before responding. You may want to start with some general comments and then get specific. Topics to cover include:

- Describe current performance. In what ways is current performance not meeting your expectations? Be prepared to provide one or more specific examples.
- Explain the business consequences of current performance—Late deliveries? Upset customers? Poor quality? Unhappy employees? It is very important that people understand the full consequences of their behavior.
- Gain agreement. Does the employee agree that there is a problem? You can't move on to solutions until there is agreement on the problem.
- Discuss suggestions for improvement.

Any one of the management styles discussed in chapter 3—directing, discussing, and delegating—can be used to deliver the message. The directing style may be appropriate when the employee has violated an important policy or regulation. In some cases, a directing style is effective at breaking through people's defenses.

Utilizing the discussing style, the manager makes a few comments and asks lots of questions. The right question can help employees discover for themselves what changes are needed.

Using the delegating style, a manager might say to an employee, "I want you to think about today's customer meeting. Identify what worked well and what needs improvement."

Whatever delivery approach you use, it's important to express confidence in the person's ability to change. If you don't have confidence in the individual, don't waste your time giving feedback.

The individual may need some type of support to change their behavior. Support can run the gamut from encouragement and mentoring to training and development. Be clear on what support you're willing to provide.

Every meeting must produce action items. End the meeting by reviewing the action items and due dates. Establish a follow-up date to discuss progress. "I'd like to meet with you in two weeks to review your action items."

Timing
When will the feedback have the best chance of making an impact? Timing is an important consideration for both the sender and receiver. Feedback is most effective when both parties are open and undivided attention is given. A former vice president at The Travelers states, "Make sure you have the time and 'focused attention' to discuss the issue. A hurried conversation will dilute the message. However, timing is seldom perfect." Managers can improve their timing by doing the following:

- Take advantage of "teachable moments." These are times when people are most open to receiving feedback. In my experience these often occur after a major success or failure.

- Ask permission. Simply ask the person, "Are you open to some feedback on…?" Naturally, as a manager you have the position power to make people hear you out. But will they listen? Asking permission says to the employee, "I want to make sure you're ready, willing, and able to handle some criticism." Asking permission also creates a bit of curiosity in the employee.
- Schedule a meeting. Find a mutually convenient time to discuss the feedback.

The timing of the feedback message is important. A "good" message delivered at the wrong time will have minimal impact.

Set the Example
As a manager, it's important to set a positive example when receiving feedback. Don't get defensive. Listen carefully to the message before responding. Ask the person to clarify any comments you don't understand.

Summary
Continuous improvement requires effective feedback. In essence, feedback helps people identify <u>what</u> needs to change and <u>how</u> to accomplish better results. Without feedback it's "business as usual."

Applying the Concept

Pam Cavanaugh, President and CEO, Cavanaugh Leahy & Company

If providing feedback to an employee is viewed as a confrontation, it will be just that. A requirement for quality feedback is for a manager to care enough about his/her people to acknowledge them for their contributions and capabilities as well as providing feedback on needed improvements (focusing on what's missing in performance as distinct from what's wrong). If a manager has created a learning environment where an employee knows that he/she is valued and trusted, feedback will be welcomed.

Applying the Concept

Phil Beaudoin, Managing Partner, Be The Leader Associates

For several years, I conducted a five-session program dedicated to improving the ability of people to make effective presentations. Participants were usually there because they wanted to be and thus were open to feedback. The seminar focused on how to plan, organize and deliver an effective business presentation.

Prior to each presentation, participants were asked what specific areas that I would use to provide feedback such as making eye contact, using gestures, or handling questions from the audience. This helped me focus in on the target areas. Most of the time I'd wait for the presenter to finish before launching into the feedback portion, unless there was a glaring need for just-in-time attention. Presenters were asked to first give a self-assessment. Then I provided my observations and suggestions. Videotaping was also used to support the substance of the feedback. In most cases, improvements were significant because the feedback was focused, immediate, and the person was open to receiving it.

This approach is easily transferred to business situations. Set it up so people know what they will be measured against and periodically ask them what skills or areas should be used to focus the feedback. Also, indicate when the feedback will be provided. In this way people are directly involved in defining the areas needing improvement. The challenge for every manager is to provide feedback in a way that is helpful to the receiver. Most people are willing to listen to suggestions for improvement especially in areas where they want to improve.

Chapter 13
The What, When, and How of Controls

Many textbooks define management as the process of getting things done with and through others. The key management functions include planning, organizing, decision-making, motivating and controlling. Somehow the "control" function has developed a bad reputation. "Control" has been misinterpreted as meaning micro-management, tightly monitoring everything people do.

The control function involves getting feedback to compare accomplishments to plans and then making appropriate adjustments as needed. A director of operations states, "Control has to do with getting the right information to the right people at the right time. Effective control systems help people correct problems. Employees must believe the data's accurate and complete, and they have power to improve results."

Managers need to determine:

- What information is needed? What should be measured?
- When is the information needed? When should measurements be taken?
- How should the measurements be made?

What to Measure
Measure what's important to your stakeholders—customers, stockholders and employees. Some of the most common things that are measured include quantity, quality, cost and timeliness.

Measure the key drivers that produce the desired result. Think about cause and effect. What are the causes producing the desired effect? A manager states, "Identify the driving forces that produce your competitive advantage. Measure the key variables that help you design, develop and deliver better products and services than the competition."

Don't try to measure too many things. Most experts recommend having between three and seven measures. I read about one company that measured over 130 different things. It's impossible to stay focused on that many items. What you measure tells employees what's important. If you try to measure everything, then nothing becomes important.

When to measure
How often is feedback needed? Daily? Weekly? Monthly? Quarterly? It depends on several factors such as the priority of the task, the person's experience level, and what makes sense in terms of major milestones. For example, a professor might monitor students' performance after each section of the book has been covered.

"When to measure" also has to do with your level in the organization. First line supervisors may keep daily metrics, while a middle manager may only need to receive feedback on a weekly or monthly basis.

Should you measure before, during, or after the event? The following types of controls are appropriate depending on when feedback is needed.

- Concurrent controls—These controls measure performance minute by minute. For example, while in intensive care, a person's vital signs are monitored continuously. Observing people perform their job is another example of concurrent controls.
- Feedback controls—This type of control provides feedback after something has been completed. For example, budget reports provide feedback on what was spent after the fact. Feedback controls measure history by pointing out what happened in the past.
- Preventive controls—This type of control takes place prior to the performance of an activity. For example, carpenters have their own version of preventive control: "Measure twice, cut once."

How to measure
Three of the most basic ways to measure include observations, manually collected data, and system generated data.

- Observation—Visually monitor what's happening or what has been completed. All military personnel have learned that after an order is given, the officer in charge needs to go out and see for himself whether it has been carried out.
- Manually collected data—count the number of widgets produced, calls completed, or sales made.
- System generated data—increasingly information systems are being used to collect, store and provide feedback.

There is a cost associated with each approach. Obviously you don't want to spend $1000 to control a $10 transaction. It's also important to determine the degree of accuracy needed. Precise measures aren't always needed. Subjective measures of customer satisfaction may be appropriate and sufficient.

Interrelationships
Controls that provide the right information at the wrong time don't help managers achieve organizational goals. In addition, controls that provide the right information at the right time but cost an exorbitant amount of money are ineffective.

Summary
Control is an essential management function. The purpose of the controls is to get the job done despite obstacles, problems, and uncertainties that occur.

Applying the Concept

Mary Jean Thornton, former Executive Vice President & CIO, The Travelers Life and Annuity Company

I led a large organization, approximately 800 people. At the macro level, the controls I used included budgets, head count, risks and milestones on major strategic initiatives. Each of my direct reports had more specific controls for the area they managed. For example, in the "servicing area" we measured productivity, quality, expenses, cycle time, and customer satisfaction.

<u>What to measure/control</u>--You need to identify the specific drivers that will produce the desired output. Control the three to five

things that are vital to the business. Determine your current baseline. Establish goals of where you need to be. Implement improvement plans and monitor results. But you also need to get feedback on the "soft measures." Look underneath the numbers. By that I mean get informal feedback from employees, customers, and other stakeholders. The numbers don't always tell you the whole story.

<u>*When to measure/control*</u>—*It depends on your level in the organization. A first-line supervisor could measure results daily. A middle manager may receive feedback weekly. Controls for a strategic initiative might only be needed monthly or even quarterly. Your objective is to get feedback in time to make corrections or changes as needed. Of course, when performance problems occur, tighter controls are implemented.*

<u>*How to control/measure*</u>—*It's great if you can have your computer network collect the data and provide feedback as needed. It's important to have integrity in the numbers. In addition, there must be agreement to use one information source. When groups or departments start to track their own numbers, it produces chaos. If you don't have a computer system, start with some simple measures and build from there.*

Good controls are critical. Your ability to determine problems and recover by effecting change is directly related to your control system.

Chapter 14
The Finance Triangle

What do the numbers mean? Some managers feel insecure when it comes to challenging the numbers presented by the accountants and financial analysts. They have made the numbers more mysterious and confusing than they really are.

Numbers are the measures—the scorecard of what's going on in each area. The financial numbers are the raw material of budgets, balance sheets and income statements. A senior manager states, "Financial measures are like the gauges on the dashboard of your car. They measure what's going on. The feedback helps you focus, take action, and make adjustments as needed."

Tim Still, Vice President, Annuity Servicing, The Travelers, states, "Companies have three basic goals: 1. Increase sales; 2. Reduce expenses; and 3. Increase operating profit." Managers need to understand the relationships between and among these three variables.

- Profit
- Sales
- Expenses

When analyzing each variable, it's important to understand both the numbers that describe the current situation and the trend—how those numbers have changed over time. For example, a manager might find the current cost of item X is $24. The six-month trend indicates that the cost has increased by $4.50. The current cost and trend data are both important pieces of the puzzle.

Profit

It's the famous "bottom line." Profit is good; the more, the better. The word "profit" comes from the Latin word profectus, meaning advancement or improvement. Profitable companies have the money to reward people, invest in new technology, and develop new products. An executive remarks, "People want to be part of a successful company. One measure of success is making a profit."

Start-up companies often lose money their first one to three years of operation. However, you can't go on losing money for long. Unfortunately, many internet companies didn't think this rule applied to them.

Profits measure two things:

1. The extent to which customers buy your products and services.
2. How efficiently the business produces and delivers the products and services.

One manager states, "At the top of my 'to-do list' are the action items that will increase sales and reduce cost. Both impact profit. It's the difference between sales and expenses that is the true measure of success."

Making a profit is important. Companies make the point very clear when they implement profit-sharing programs. When 20% of your compensation is based on profit, it motivates you to work smarter and harder. Great efforts are taken to eliminate waste and unnecessary expenses. Profit-sharing focuses people's attention on all three variables—sales, expenses and profit.

Sales

More sales equals more profits, assuming you make some profit on each dollar of sales. How do companies increase sales? They do one or more of the following:

- Increase sales of current products to current customers.
- Increase their customer base.
- Develop new products and services for current and/or new customers.
- Increase the number of uses for their product.

The approach you take to increase sales ties back to your mission and vision. What's your business purpose and where are you going? (See Chapter 1.)

Growth in your top line from sales shows that customers are increasingly valuing your products. However, many companies grow their costs as quickly as their sales, so they don't profit. The best companies learn to increase sales volume without increasing fixed costs.

The best companies are continuously improving their processes to identify, develop and sell great products. Here are a few things they do:

- Observe customers. Ask questions. What problems do they have? What new products would make their lives easier?

- Brainstorm. Generate lots of new ideas. Ask "what if" questions. Always be searching for the next big idea.
- Simplify. Make it easy for customers to understand in what ways your products are different and better than the competition.
- Make it easy to buy your products and services.
- Give yourself a phone call. Experience what your customers experience.

Bottom line—managers must constantly look for and find ways to increase sales.

Expenses
Think of expenses as costs incurred to produce and sell products and services. First, you need to understand the sources of all costs. Companies that have the best success in cutting costs focus on the right target areas. In addition, they simplify and improve their processes so new costs don't show up elsewhere in the organization.

Bob Fifer, author of *Double Your Profit,* maintains that there are two types of costs:

- Strategic costs—all the things done to bring in new business such as advertising, sales reps and promotional programs.
- Non-strategic costs—all the costs necessary to run the business such as rent, utilities, and office supplies.

His philosophy is to spend more than the competition on strategic costs. But don't waste money; spend it on the "right things." Ruthlessly cut non-strategic costs to the bone. Cutting costs—budget cuts and downsizing—isn't fun work but it is necessary.

Profits can be equally impacted by increasing sales or by cutting costs. Managers would prefer to spend their time thinking about spending money to improve the business.

Eliminating costs starts with having the right mindset. For example, have the attitude that <u>there are no such things as "fixed costs.</u>" This arbitrary designation conveys the meaning that a "fixed cost" can't be reduced. Not true. All costs can be eliminated or reduced.

Here are a few suggestions on cutting costs:

- Before hiring additional people, analyze your current staff's productivity.
- Eliminate all unnecessary reports, procedures and meetings. In every organization there is some amount of waste.
- Cut budgets aggressively. If you cut too far, you always have opportunities to correct your mistakes. On the other hand, if you spend too much, that money is gone forever.
- Attack the price you pay suppliers.
- The R&D budget can't be a sacred cow. The question needs to be—how effectively is the money being spent? Is it leading to new products customers will buy?
- Reduce inventory. As inventories are reduced, you need less space and fewer people to manage the inventory. You free up money that was previously tied up in inventory.

Bottom line— managers must constantly look for and find ways to cut costs. Mike Tenerowicz, professor and small business advisor, states, " I'm constantly telling clients to answer these questions before making any purchase: Will this purchase help you increase sales? Will this purchase make your business run more efficiently?"

Relationships (Ratios)
Ratios simply show the relationship between two things. Within each of the variables (sales, costs and profit) there are a number of factors that can be compared. Here are a few examples:

Sales
- Sales/Employee
- Average sales/Customer
- Sales of product A/Sales of product B
- Net sales/Assets

Be curious. What relationships will provide new insights and ideas regarding sales? Ratios help you see the connections between various components of sales.

Costs
- Fixed/Variable
- Material/Labor
- Benefits/Direct labor

There are many cost relationships that may be of interest to you. The objective is to calculate ratios that will help you gain a fuller understanding of cost variables.

Profits
- Sales/Service
- Product A/Product B
- Net Income/Net sales

Where does profit come from? What products or projects are generating the most profit?

Other ratios that are often used to analyze a business include:

- **Quick Assets/Current Liabilities** Quick assets are cash and accounts receivable. This ratio indicates the ability to pay current bills.
- **Profits/Sales** This ratio indicates the relationship between profit and sales. It answers the question, "For each dollar of sales, how much profit is generated?"
- **Debt/Equity** This ratio shows the relationship between the amount of money provided by creditors and the assets being provided by the owners of the business.

Note that some ratios must go up to be good, others need to go down to indicate a positive trend.

Summary
Keep your eyes clearly focused on sales, expenses and profit. These three variables are interconnected. It's important for managers to understand the trend data and various ratios that give insight into what's happening between and among these variables.

Applying the Concept

Chris Manolakis, President, Abbett Business Services, Inc.

My company provides finance and accounting services to approximately 60 businesses. A key part of my job is advising business owners on what to do to impact the bottom line.

Increase sales—I tell my clients to view their business as a "V". The bottom of the "V" represents their core products and services.

You have to stay grounded in what you do well, but also look for new ways to help your customers. Another way to increase sales is through co-branding. If you run a gas station or convenience store, consider leasing out space for a Dunkin Donuts, Blimpie's or Subway operation. This can be a win-win deal.

Managing expenses—People who start a business often struggle, sacrifice, and scrape by for a year or two. When sales start to take off there is an entitlement attitude— "I sacrificed, I'm entitled to a new computer, secretary, car, office, etc." That's a dangerous attitude. Expenses can grow quickly. Little expenses can get overlooked once you start making some money. I had a client whose long distance phone charges had grown to 62 cents per minute. With some negotiations the business owner was able to reduce it to 7 cents per minute. Managers need to realize scrap, rework, and pilferage impact your expenses. If you're operating on a small profit margin think about how much you have to sell to make up for a $50 loss. Constantly look for ways to cut expenses, but don't cut the wrong expenses. Spend money on things that generate sales and lead to profits.

I coach business owners to keep a focused eye on both sales and expenses.

Applying the Concept

Steve Topor, Vice President and General Manager, Unisource

Unisource is a national distribution company with divisions in all major markets in the United States. We serve a broad cross-section of businesses with three principle product lines that include printing & imaging paper, industrial packaging supplies, and facility supplies. As a general manager, I have P&L responsibility for the division in northern California.

As part of our income planning process we have targets for each corner of the finance triangle—sales, expenses, and profit. In order to achieve a given increase in profit, we need to drive it with additional sales and a limited amount of additional expense. This process helps clarify the type of customer we must pursue. "Any customer is a good customer" isn't true. A $100 order from the local gas station isn't what we're after. Our cost structure and business model require that we target large customers who generate large orders.

The sales function is responsible for driving sales growth by hiring, training, and motivating our sales force. Our compensation structure is designed to reward sales reps for growth. There are additional incentives that promote the growth of certain products that generate higher profit margins. These tactics are used to motivate reps to reach their goals and the company goals. Once we have customer orders, the operations function is responsible for the assembly and delivery of the products. Our costs are based largely on warehouse and driver staffing levels, the productivity and quality of their work, and the cost to operate our fleet. All of these costs are closely managed.

Operating profit is very sensitive to changes in sales and/or expenses. As sales change up or down, corresponding changes must be made on the expense side of the equation. Otherwise we will not achieve desired profit levels. We have a system called "dashboard indicators" (like the dials on your car dashboard that measure speed, fuel, mileage, etc.) to monitor the "vital few" factors that have the most significant impact on the bottom line.

THE TRIANGLES OF MANAGEMENT AND LEADERSHIP

NBA coaches enter each contest with specific goals and a game plan. As the game unfolds, they make many adjustments based on factors, such as what plays are working and not working, player fouls, turnovers, and who's scoring. In a similar way, I need specific goals and a game plan for sales, expenses and profit. As the year unfolds, I have to make the right adjustments to be successful.

Chapter 15
Dealing with Difficult People

"He's driving me crazy!"

Managers deal with a wide range of personalities. Most people are cooperative and reasonable. However, some employees are very difficult to be around and work with. A human resources manager states, "They're totally focused on their own agenda and needs. They cause tension and conflicts. Difficult people absorb a lot of a manager's time and attention."

Three types of difficult people are:

- The aggressor
- The victim
- The rescuer

You may never "like" these people. But it is important that you understand them and develop techniques to help them be more productive.

The Aggressor
Aggressive people are demanding and loud. They don't listen and they talk over people. Their attitude is, "I'm right, you're wrong."

Their view of the world is win/lose, and of course, they must "win." Some of the words used to describe aggressive people include: "Sherman tank," "bull in the china shop," and "bullies." A participant in one of my seminars commented, "Aggressive people talk down to people. They're know-it-alls. They make rude comments, followed by biting sarcasm."

Some of the comments I've heard aggressive people make include:

- "If you don't like it, leave. It's my way or the highway."
- "You don't know what you're talking about. I'm right."
- "Drop whatever you're doing –I need this completed ASAP."

When dealing with aggressive people, start by letting them vent. They often are angry and need to blow off steam. Use active listening skills to indicate you're trying to understand their views. Aggressive people aren't used to people really listening to them. Most often it's point, counterpoint, reload, and attack again.

Sometimes it's hard to get a word in when the aggressor is verbally attacking. Try "clipping." This technique allows you to get a few words in such as "Yes," "No," "I agree," "No, you're wrong." This often causes the attacker to back off and take a breath.

Aggressive people are often tolerated because they do get things done. The problem is that they also cause tension and upset people. In addition, because they dominate the conversation, other people don't contribute, which results in lost input.

Aggressive people need to realize there is more than one right answer. Their opinions are valid and valued, but other people have equally valid ideas.

The Victim

Harvard researchers Robert Kegan and Lisa Laskow Lahey describe victims as "BMW" people. They bitch, whine and moan. They blame others for their problems and come across as timid and helpless. Their attitude is, "People don't understand how bad I have it." A student in one of my courses said, "Victims are depressing to be around. They feel sorry for themselves and blow problems out of proportion. They waste a lot of time and don't take any responsibility for making changes."

Victims like to "blamestorm." They're very good at discovering reasons and finding people to "blame" for their performance shortfalls. Their stories and explanations are purposefully incomplete. They leave out the details that indicate their inability to get the job done.

Some of the comments I've heard victims make include:

- "Why does this always happen to me?"
- "I can't get it done. I never have time for myself."
- "They won't give me the information I need."

When dealing with "victims" take the time to listen to their complaints. A middle manager states, "Victims complain so much, no one really takes the time to listen to them. They feel neglected." Feed back your understanding of what the victim has said. Try to force the victim to prioritize his or her problems. Next, facilitate a discussion to help him/her choose an appropriate course of action to solve the problem.

Victims need to realize they are not helpless. Find ways to help them achieve some short-term wins. A colleague states, "Victims have strong psychological needs for attention and recognition.

THE TRIANGLES OF MANAGEMENT AND LEADERSHIP

Recognize them for taking responsibility and achieving success, not for winning."

The Rescuer
The rescuer is the person who's always willing to help other people. Their major need is to be liked and appreciated. "I'll help" are their favorite words. Rescuers are very good at recognizing when other people need help, and they know how to jump in to save the day. A consultant friend remarks, "The rescuer avoids confrontation. They're 'yes' people. They say 'yes' without thinking through the implications. Oftentimes they overcommit and their own work doesn't get done."

Some of the comments I've heard rescuers make include:

- "I hesitated to fire non-performers. I was afraid of ruining someone's life. It was my responsibility to take care of people."
- "I habitually took care of other people's problems."
- "I know this is your project, but let me add it to my list to take the burden off of you."

When dealing with rescuers it's important to hold them accountable to performing all of their job responsibilities. If they have excess capacity the manager should assign them bigger bricks to carry.

Interrelationships
Aggressive people find, and sometimes create victims. Victims are easy prey for the bully. Victims don't get the job done but always have excuses why it's not their fault. Rescuers jump in to save the victim. Everyone wins! This cycle can go round and round, each

playing his/her role and in effect supporting the behavior of the other two.

You can do several things when dealing with difficult people.
1. Listen to them. Let them know you want to understand their point of view.
2. Make them feel valued and appreciated.
3. Have them read this chapter. Indicate we all play these roles to some degree. Ask them which role they play most often. Discuss the impact that role has on others.
4. Indicate what you would like to see them do more of and less of.
5. Ask them to commit to making one or two changes.

Summary
Dealing with difficult people is a challenge. However it's possible to help them be more productive and effective in doing their job.

Applying the Concept

Jim Ligotti, Senior Technical Manager, Sikorsky Aircraft

First and foremost, I try to get an understanding of what's driving the person's behavior. It's also important to remain calm and communicate openly with difficult people. Aggressive people are looking to be recognized and rewarded. I work with the person to help him see the fastest way he can achieve his goals. Aggressive people produce negative vibes, which impacts their ability to be successful. Co-workers don't go the extra mile to help irritating people. I try to help aggressive people make that connection. Less aggression and more cooperation goes a long way.

The issue with victims is that they believe they cannot get the whole task completed, because inevitably something will be outside their control. This makes me think of elephant training. The young elephant is restrained by one leg. While elephants are young and not very strong, they are unable to get free. Over time elephants become conditioned. When they are older and stronger and could get free, they don't even try. Their attitude is, why try now; it's never worked before. This is similar to the victim. The key is to retrain them. They have to believe they can control their destiny. Help them develop a new, positive, can-do attitude. Help them plan and achieve short term wins. As they learn and "win," increase their field of influence.

Rescuers want to help their teammates but often don't see the negative effects of missed commitments. I try to help these people realize that offering to help and missing their own commitments is worse than not offering at all. Rescuers have to learn to focus first on their own commitments. Sometimes it helps to show rescuers how to prioritize and manage their time effectively.

Dealing with difficult people is an investment in time. These people are executing "learned" behaviors. I coach and mentor them on more effective ways to reach their goals. It takes time to build trust. However, when people truly believe you're trying to help them succeed, they listen and respond.

Applying the Concept

William H. Denney, Ph.D., Quality Consultant

<u>Aggressor</u>
Hold your ground. Don't change your position out of intimidation.

Interrupt by saying their name until they stop to listen. Go back and clarify their first point. Slows them down and shows you are listening.
Only address the key issue and don't get tangled up in miscellaneous stuff.
Don't piss them off and embarrass them. Give them a way out. Seek a win-win if possible.
If you are in the right position, don't be afraid to fire an aggressor that is damaging teamwork. Regardless of technical skill and or hard work, aggressors can demoralize and destroy a company.

If the aggressor is your boss then that's another story. You have to figure out if he/she is a detail person or a big picture person and give them what they are most comfortable with.

Victim
Listen and empathize.
Ask for specifics that you can analyze and comment on, or correct wrong perceptions.
Focus on solutions and the future, not the past.
If necessary, draw a line in the sand and tell them that talking about complaints without solutions is unproductive and time wasting.
Don't be afraid to tell them they are undermining company success by affecting the morale of others.
Offer to help them find another job.

Rescuer
The rescuer is more of a "know-it-all."
Be prepared for your discussions with this person. They think they know more than you and others.

THE TRIANGLES OF MANAGEMENT AND LEADERSHIP

Be appreciative, respectful and sincere about their contribution.
Take an indirect approach to help them see your point to avoid putting them on the defensive.
Use soft words -- maybe, perhaps, we, us, etc.
Help them understand that there is time for others to have a learning curve on what needs to be done.
Help them understand that it is in the company's interest to have more knowledge in the pipe line.
Use them as a coach to others if possible.
If you are in a position to do so, get them into team training. Even facilitator training will enlighten their views and show them how to work with others.

Advice on dealing with difficult people
Everyone means well. Listen and understand before you try to give your opinion or position.
Try to determine what circumstance in the past has molded their position.
Repeat without agreeing so they know you understand their concerns.
Get their input on how to improve the situation. Pass it along or act on it if possible.
Strive for a win-win situation. There is often a middle ground.
If nothing works, don't let them undermine morale. Offer to help them find another job.

Chapter 16
Introducing and Managing Change

I love change! I hate change!

Today's complex business environment requires rapid change. New technology, changed work processes, increased customer expectations, and new relationships between employees are common.

Changes we initiate are viewed as positive adventures. For example, I look forward to dining at a new restaurant or exploring a seaside resort. However, we resist changes that are thrust upon us. A middle manager commented, "Forced change can produce a range of emotions, including hope, excitement, anxiety, defensiveness, and fear. People's reaction to change is complex. One thing for sure, leadership and change go hand in hand."

Change initiatives can be focused at the individual, group or organizational level. Leaders take the following three steps to introduce and manage change.

- Create the need
- Define the specific required change
- Support the change

Create the need

After a heart attack, most people are open to change. They're willing to stop smoking, start dieting, and exercising. Before initiating a business change leaders must "create the need" for change. Otherwise it's, "Why change? I know how to do my job." Many people like staying in their comfort zone. In there it's safe, secure and predictable. Change often involves going from the known to the unknown. Fear of the unknown keeps people close to their comfort zone.

Leaders must be able to explain and convince people that change is needed. An executive at a Fortune 100 company said, "If you can't articulate the business case for change, you're stuck in neutral. It's business as usual." What's the major reason change is needed? The competition keeps improving. A management consultant states, "Every day the competition gets smarter, faster, and more efficient. If you're not learning and taking steps to improve your process, you're dead meat."

The objective is to increase people's openness, readiness, and capacity to change and improve. The following actions help create the need for change:

- State your vision. Remind people of what's possible. Contrast current reality (what is) with the desired future state (what could be).
- Ask "what if" questions. "What if" questions plant seeds for people to consider new ideas. "What if we eliminate the procedure entirely?" "What if we outsource the HR function?"
- Constantly ask "why." Asking "why" forces people to think through the logic and assumptions behind current practices. "Why do we use this manufacturing process?"

- Find and circulate articles that describe best practices. Show how other organizations are achieving excellence.
- Benchmark. Visit leading organizations. Stew Leonard's Dairy in Norwalk, Connecticut regularly takes groups of employees on "One Idea Field Trips." They travel to other supermarkets, and each employee is expected to find one new idea he will use back on his job.
- Get customer feedback. On a regular basis, ask customers what they like and dislike. Customers' expectations keep increasing. What was "great" yesterday is "average" today.
- Ask for consideration. Sometimes the most straightforward thing to do is simply ask employees to consider a potential new approach. "I'd like you to consider a new work schedule."
- Describe the carrots. People want to know "What's in it for me?" The right incentive gets people's attention.

Effective leaders use a variety of techniques to "create the need." In addition, they don't view "creating the need" as a once and done activity. The need for continuous improvement and the changes that implies are discussed frequently.

Leaders sometimes stage symbolic acts to stress the need for change. For example, one leader put all the company policy manuals in a pile and then set it on fire. The message: the old rules no longer apply, it's a new ballgame.

Leaders need to identify and encourage people who support the change initiative. Provide opportunities for them to voice their support. But, expect resistance. I've found that about 20 to 30% of the people resist almost any change. Listen to people's concerns and the reasons why they think change is not needed. Resisters may have some valid points that need to be evaluated. When resisters feel their views are heard and understood, they're more likely to listen to other points of view.

Many change efforts fail because the "need for change" was never firmly established. Without the <u>need</u> there's no motivation to do things differently.

Define the Required Change
What change is needed? Do you want people to think differently? Have a different attitude? Behave differently?

Some change initiatives don't succeed because it's unclear what specific changes are desired. I've heard company presidents say things like:

- "...our organization needs to be more customer focused."
- "Teamwork is critical for our success."

Employees heard the message but weren't sure what actions to take. In some cases employees thought they already were "customer focused" and a "team player."

My advice is to show people what the desired behavior looks like. Give them an example. What does "customer focus" look like? Being able to see the desired behaviors takes the mystery and guesswork out of what's expected.

Be specific. "Here's what your new job responsibilities will be after the reorganization." Set goals and deadlines that tie directly to the change initiative. Since change involves new responsibilities and ways of working, it follows that there should also be new measures to track progress. Let people know what will be measured and why it's important. Provide frequent feedback, especially during the early phase of change.

If the desired change is clear and specific, there is a much higher probability people will succeed.

Support the Change
Change doesn't just happen. It needs to be nurtured. Expect problems and frustrations especially during the initial implementation. When the "rubber meets the road," it can be bumpy. There are always potholes and problems along the way. Some people will react with fears and doubts. "I don't think I can learn the new software." "I don't know how I'm going to handle being on three teams."

"Support" can take several forms:

- Psychological support. Help people deal with their doubts and fears. Build people's confidence. Affirm their talents and determination to succeed. Remind people of their previous successes.
- Training support. Help people learn the "how-to-do-it" part of the equation. Change usually requires new knowledge and skills. Provide the target audience with the appropriate education and training. Help people use and apply their new skills.
- Cheerleading support. Provide frequent recognition and rewards for people's efforts and accomplishments. Plan and celebrate short-term wins. Momentum will increase if there are positive results early on.

Perhaps the biggest way leaders support the change is by setting the example. Practice what you preach. Stay positive, engaged, and determined to succeed. When leaders lose focus, become negative, and don't "walk the talk," the change initiative is doomed.

Summary
Leaders know change is required to stay competitive. They not only create the need for change, but also show people what to do and how to do it. When this is done, employees gain confidence, face reality and adopt the continuous improvement mindset. Leaders energize people to change, grow and be their best.

Applying the Concept

Eric Hatch, Ph.D., President, Hatch Organizational Consulting

The first thing you need to do is define the business reality that is dictating the change so that people see it, feel it, and understand it. One case in point was a merger between two very hostile and different cultures. The need was to get along together and forge something new; this was communicated through an Open Space event. (These events bring together the largest and most representative chunk of the affected organization for a very open-ended series of meetings to address key issues.)

Working with another client, we articulated the need for change by conducting a series of exercises that said, in effect, "here's what you say are your strategy and your long-term goal. What are the characteristics of such a company?" It wasn't hard to do a gap analysis showing the areas in which change was essential in order to bring the preferred future back to the present.

What have I learned about implementing change? First and most important is the need to get the infrastructure (policies, procedures, approval cycles, employee manuals) OUT OF THE WAY. The actual observed data from Jeff Fierstein's studies show that operational change precedes infrastructure change. However, I believe that going after the infrastructure stuff IMMEDIATELY, even if you get it wrong, accelerates change.

Another thing is to let the sustaining sponsors of change have the authority to say "yes." If everything they or senior change agents do has to run up to the top of the mountain to be blessed, nothing will really change.

The third thing is DON'T START A CHANGE UNLESS YOU'RE PREPARED TO LIVE WITH THE CONSEQUENCES. We had a client that swore up and down he wanted to create a participative, team-oriented organization, while all the people he hired were used to internally-competing organizations. He himself continued to act exactly as he always had. The organization fell apart in less than six months and had no resilience when hard times came along.

Frequently leaders think they want a change and when they realize that change will cost them some level of control, they chicken out and back away, leaving people cynical and doubtful. So my advice is "ask what it's going to be like around here once you've gone through this change. Is it a place you'll want to work?"

Finally, it's important to build a network of cascading sponsorship reaching down to, and investing, the "thought leaders" of the organization. They're the people who have to latch on to the new process or method, and when they do, others will follow. Identifying, enrolling, and sustaining such people is a vital step.

Applying the Concept

Mark Breier, Managing Partner, Fast Angels Ventures (www.fastangels.com) and former Vice President, Marketing, Amazon.com
Author of "The 10-Second Internet Manager"
(*www.10secondmanager.com*)

Two very good examples of how to introduce and manage change occurred when I was at Amazon.com.

1) Setting a *"big, hairy audacious goal"* (BHAG, as Jim Collins has coined it) can be one way to get everybody around change. Jeff Bezos researched who the fastest company to $10b in revenue was (Costco and Home Depot) and then showed how, if Amazon.com entered 5 categories and grew the customer base over the next 3 years, we could set the record. Also, he explained how someone on the internet was bound to do it faster than the land-based companies who need to buy/rent real estate. It was a big, hairy goal, on the one hand, but eminently doable via the internet on the other.

2) Getting different department heads "bought in" on a new direction can be a challenge. Jeff Bezos simply put them all on the launch team and had a junior director send around a plan to get their input into and get their signatures on the final going-to-market document! Once you've signed a public release date and plan, you're part of the team.

Chapter 17
The Triangles of Leading Teams

Good teams don't just happen!

Seven people are waiting to take the elevator to the eighteenth floor. They have a common goal and strategy. Are they a team? No!

A team is a small number of people who are committed to working together to achieve desired results. Certainly team members need a common commitment to specific goals and strategies. But, in addition, team members must effectively "work together"—that's the essence of teamwork. Working together means talking, sharing ideas, challenging assumptions, debating issues, establishing goals, making decisions, and dealing with changing priorities.

It's difficult for team members to consistently work together in a highly productive manner. Hidden agendas, hurt feelings and interpersonal conflicts often develop. Some team members don't feel valued or don't feel their ideas are given full consideration. Teams can lose their focus and make little progress.

What makes a team successful? When I'm assessing a team I focus on the following questions:

- Do team members have a clear understanding of what needs to be accomplished?
- Do people on the team have the required knowledge and skills?
- Have team members established rules to work by? Are the rules followed and enforced?

The team leader plays a major role in helping team members work together and achieve the desired goals. The triangle of leading teams includes the following three factors:

- Deliverables (output)
- People (team members)
- Rules

Deliverables
What does the team need to produce? What are the deliverables? Christopher M. Avery, Ph.D. states, "Get clear on the collective task. Teambuilding starts with clarifying your team's purpose, not with getting your teammates to like each other. After all, the task itself—not the people performing the task—is the reason the team was created." Generally the person or group that charters a team defines what the team must accomplish. However, sometimes the person chartering the team isn't crystal clear in describing what needs to be accomplished.

Some of the most common outputs or deliverables teams are assigned include:

- Define a problem or frame an opportunity
- Establish specific goals and objectives
- Recommend alternatives to solve a problem or to take advantage of a new opportunity

- Do a cost/benefit analysis of each alternative
- Select the "best" alternative
- Develop an implementation plan
- Implement the plan
- All of the above

As you can see there are many reasons why teams are created. If the team charter isn't clear the results will miss the mark. Even with a clear charter, some teams lose their focus. One team leader I know starts each team meeting with an overhead slide that describes the team's mission, key deliverables and due dates. He says this is a constant reminder of the task that needs to be completed.

Team leaders need task skills. Effective team leaders are able to break down a large project into bite size pieces. They're able to help the team in areas such as determining what information to gather, discussing ideas, developing plans, making decisions, assigning tasks, holding people accountable and taking all the steps necessary to achieve the desired results.

People
Who should be on the team?
- Most experts recommend the fewer people, the better—somewhere between 5 to 9 is ideal. If you have 15 people on a team it's difficult and time consuming to have all members discuss their ideas.
- People with the right mix of knowledge, skills and experiences needed for the assigned task. Most experts recommend a variety of skills such as strategic thinking, planning, problem solving, follow-up, facilitation, and detail orientation are important for team success.

- If the problem spans the total organization, you need a cross-functional team with members from department such as marketing, finance, operations, human resources and engineering.
- People who have enthusiasm, interest, and motivation.

Team leaders also need "people skills." A colleague states, "Soliciting their ideas, making people feel valued, involving all team members, smoothing out relationship issues is all part of the team leader's job description."

Rules
How will team members work together?
Effective teams develop a few rules they commit to follow. An experienced team leader says, " Develop the rules as a group, put them in writing and distribute them to all team members." Most of the time teams "work together" in meetings. A few of the rules I like to use include:

- Start and end meetings on time
- Respect all team members
- Listen and fully consider all ideas
- Complete all assigned action items
- Don't hold back; if you have something on your mind, say it.

Team leaders often use "process checks" to evaluate how well team members are working together. Process checks provide opportunities for each team member to comment on what's working and not working.

Stages of Team Development

Like any relationship between two or more people, teams go through stages. Psychologist B. W. Tuckman originally conducted research on small group interactions and described four stages of team evolution—forming, storming, norming and performing. It sounds like teams go through these stages in a neat and orderly progression. They don't. They bounce back and forth as members leave the team, new people join and the team experiences major successes and failures.

My analysis leads me to believe teams bounce between and among three stages—forming, storming, and performing. In each stage there are certain issues that must be resolved. The team leader has a major responsibility in resolving issues at each stage.

Forming

Team members meet for the first time. They communicate in a polite, tentative manner. At this point they are a collection of individuals. In the forming stage, people have questions like the following:

- Why was I selected for this team?
- How much time and effort will this require?
- What's in it for me? What can I learn?
- Who are these other people and why were they selected?
- What are they interested in?

Team members need a chance to get to know each other both formally and informally. It's important to schedule activities, such as lunches, pizza parties and an occasional after work drink. Informal, social activities provide team members with an opportunity to build and strengthen relationships.

The team leader needs to be prepared to make an introductory presentation that describes the general nature of the project, time commitments, and the benefits team members can derive.

Storming

In this stage, team members begin to have conflicts about goals, priorities and how things will be done. Team members are very interested in power, influence and assigned roles. Sometimes subgroups develop their own needs and agenda. People ask themselves questions like the following:

- How much power do I have?
- Who agrees with my point of view?
- What's their point of view?
- Who has the most influence?
- Who are my allies?
- What's my role? What's their role?

The team leader has to keep the members focused on the "team" goals and strategies. In addition, the team leader has to establish rules that give all team members equal opportunity to contribute and influence group decision-making. Assigned roles must be clarified and rotated as needed.

Performing

In this stage, team members start performing—working together. As the team works together, standards of acceptable and unacceptable behavior begin to evolve. Team members need to be clear on their roles and assigned action items. In addition, team members need frequent feedback on what's being accomplished.

Team leaders need to observe and monitor team behavior. It's important to observe to what extent team members are:

- Participating
- Following the rules
- Demonstrating motivation
- Making progress

If the team is not utilizing everyone's ideas, or not following the rules, or not achieving desired results, it's incumbent on the team leader to address those issues with the team. I was once on a team where the accepted standard was that team meeting always started 10 to15 minutes late. The team leader said nothing. The best team leaders constantly raise the bar and challenge the team to pursue excellence.

Summary
More and more work is being done by teams. The ability to build effective teams is a critical leadership skill. Team leaders have to focus both on the task to be accomplished and how team members are working together. Team leaders must use the appropriate leadership style (see chapter 2) and management style (see chapter 3) to help the team consistently achieve its best performance.

Applying the Concept

Kevin McManus, Plant Manager, DaVinci Gourmet

Over the years, I have had the opportunity to work with a variety of teams in several organizations. As a team leader, I consider the following factors as being critical for team success – openness, focus, and infrastructure.

- *Openness* I have learned that teams fail due to a lack of openness more than anything else. I want each team member to feel safe in stating his or her opinion. At the same time, I want them to be open to other points of view and to question their own personal assumptions by asking: "In what way could my assumptions be wrong?" As a team leader, I try to model being "open" to all points of view. It's important to be cognizant when people start to get defensive. When I see defensive routines emerging, I immediately challenge the group to think back over the last couple of minutes of conversation. What was actually said? What did we assume that people were trying to say? In what way could our assumptions be wrong? I have found that you have to challenge and examine this type of behavior as soon as it emerges in order to begin to interrupt what is unfortunately a normal human practice.

- *Focus* The time team members spend together must be focused to make progress in achieving the desired "deliverables." The team leader and each team member should challenge the group when they feel the discussion is unfocused and just rambling. The team should also strive to make "focus evaluation" a regular part of their team meetings. It is perhaps even more important to ensure that as a supervisor I convey a consistent, focused message whenever I interact with people. For example, each day team members present me with problems. The conversations I have and the decisions I make go a long way in revealing my focus. Only by raising my self-awareness can I get better at ensuring that I am sending my people the type of message that I really mean to send.

- *Infrastructure* A team can be focused and operate with openness and still fail to get the desired results if they are not supported by an effective team infrastructure. By that I mean *the organization must provide sufficient time for team meetings, and in particular, individual work between meetings. It's important to have meeting time built into the company's expense budgets. That indicates the type of commitment and investment the organization is willing to make. In addition, the organization must clearly state how much time it is willing to invest in people to learn and practice new team skills. If you expect people to somehow find the time for team activities on their own, while also trying to meet their other job demands, your teams will flounder and eventually die.*

Applying the Concept

Alden Davis, Business Effectiveness Consultant, Pratt & Whitney Division of United Technologies

Everything familiar about the factory was now torn up and equipment was moving everywhere; this was Day Two of a Kaizen Event and only two days were left for a miracle to happen.

For two years I traipsed the globe leading workshops which taught the concepts of World Class Manufacturing. Success rested on the ability to create functional teams equipped with new concepts and compelling visions. The principles of effective teams proved-out regardless of the culture in which we were working.

Within a two-week period 40 individuals would go from strangers with no unified purpose to an interdependent group of people capable of delivering double digit performance improvements. And this would happen month after month. First, a vision of the end-state was shared using pictures from other events so that people had a sense of what was expected. The process used to equip people with the required skills always included learning-by-doing through group assignments. This started the socialization process and built a track record of success. Meals together, commuting on buses together and evening activities reinforced the message that "we are all in this together." To break through the "storming" phase we used an experiential called "Site-Central" which allowed people to see how they individually and collectively dealt with the sharing of information and power. The group was now ready to be assigned to the five project teams addressing defined areas of the factory. As the teams were launched the final expectation of greatness was set by viewing a video of how a team of 300 people built an entire house from a dirt field in less than 4 hours.

As people settled into their defined roles and began scoping out their work, targets were negotiated and set through a daily 4pm status meeting. As power and plumbing were cut, as years of history were disturbed, as forklifts began moving equipment, how could I be sure a miracle would happen? Because of the power of teams: people knit together with a common vision, equipped with skills to achieve, driving toward clearly defined, measurable outputs on a task they believed was possible. Nothing is more rewarding or exciting to me than the achievement of the "impossible" through the collective power of individuals.

Chapter 18
Managing Your Career

Never forget-- you own your own career! A career is a chosen pursuit, or profession. It's the general course or progression of one's working life.

What are your career goals? It's difficult to say what you will be doing 10 years from today. However, you do need to be thinking about your next career move and what new projects you wish to take on.

Effective career management requires the following:

- Good performance. Do more than your job description requires. Take on difficult and visible assignments. Help your boss and business succeed.
- Reflection and assessment. What do you like to do? Dislike? How do you work best? How often do you do a self-assessment of your needs, values and work performance? How often do you get performance feedback your from boss, subordinates, colleagues, and customers?
- Understanding trends in the marketplace. How are customer's needs changing? How are jobs changing? What new technologies are emerging?

- Ongoing education and development. What new skills have you developed in the last six months? What have you done to expand the scope of your job duties?
- Marketing your talents. How do you present your abilities and accomplishments without being obnoxious? How effectively does your résumé tell your story?

Three important aspects of managing your career include:

- Networking
- Utilizing Mentors
- Self-promotion

Networking
Are you plugged into what's happening in your profession? Company? Industry? Other industries? A network of contacts in each of these areas can help you stay up-to-date in your profession and industry.

Robert E. Kelly, author of *How to Be a Star at Work: Nine Breakthrough Strategies You Need to Succeed*, maintains that today's jobs are very complex and change quickly. Star performers turn to others to get help. They have a network of people they use to multiply their productivity. In addition, top performers are always on the lookout for talented people to add to their network.

Networking is a systematic approach to making contacts and building and maintaining professional relationships. Your network can help in many ways including:

- Solving problems
- Pointing out best practices

- Identifying job opportunities
- Recommending articles, books and seminars

Start building your network with people you already know—family members, friends and colleagues. Build your network by attending conferences, joining associations, and taking courses. An associate states, "I've been on numerous project teams. The people I work with are now dispersed throughout the organization. Some have joined other companies. I've continued to network with many of them."

Networking isn't one-sided. It requires you to give as much as you receive. Communicate information, ideas and articles you think will be of interest to members of your network. Kelly says that networking is a barter system. Develop expertise that people need but don't currently have.

If you only talk with the same four people week after week, the advice you receive is limited. People who learn to network vastly expand their knowledge base and resources.

Utilizing Mentors
Mentoring is for the young! No, all employees can benefit from having a good mentor. With a mentor you form a close, personal relationship. I have a network of over 100 people, but I've only had three mentors in my career.

Generally a mentor is an experienced person who helps develop a protégé's abilities through advising, coaching, tutoring, providing emotional support and being a role model. He or she is an objective, outside resource. A colleague states, "A mentor is a source of information and advice you won't learn in a textbook or classroom. Mentors are good at asking the right questions to help people think through the problem and arrive at their own conclusions."

Over the past 20 years I've heard comments such as the following:

- "My mentor helped me understand the company culture—how things really work."
- "I struggled with a career choice. My mentor helped me sort through the question of whether I was running away from something or towards a good opportunity."
- "I asked my mentor to be totally honest with me. I received some tough love. It was feedback I needed to hear."

Some companies have programs where mentors are assigned. I believe it's much better to select your own mentors. Chose someone you admire, trust and is known to be a good teacher. A career counselor states, "Certainly good chemistry is important in the mentor/mentee relationship. There has to be a foundation of trust and mutual respect."

Regular communication is important to build and maintain the relationship. Once every two weeks I had lunch with my mentor. We discussed a variety of business topics and world issues. He challenged my thinking and encouraged me to take on a bigger leadership role.

Being a mentor is a rewarding experience. Comments like the following are typical. "My experience as a mentor was exhilarating. It's very rewarding to help people blossom and achieve their goals. It's like a coach watching his team win a big game."

Self-promotion
You may be a star, but who knows about your talents and accomplishments? Many of us were taught to be modest about our abilities and accomplishments. "Don't brag. Let someone else describe what a great job you did." The only problem with that approach is you're empowering someone else to market your successes.

A key part of managing your career is letting people know what you have done and can do. Kathy Bornheimer says that people who are too quiet about letting the right people know about their abilities and accomplishments often are overlooked for great jobs or projects.

To be a good promoter you must believe in the product—namely you—your abilities and talents. You can't be lukewarm about the product. In today's competitive business world, conviction and passion are essential.

Keep a running list of your accomplishments and skills. Maintain a portfolio that includes examples of your best work. Make sure your résumé is professional and up-to-date. Prepare and perfect your elevator speech. You have two minutes to convince a senior manager to select you for an important assignment. What would you say?

Watch good sales representatives. They're able to sell a product's features and benefits in a clear, concise and convincing way. You have to be able to sell your talents.

Interrelationships
Increasing your network also increases your pool of potential mentors. In addition, as you network and utilize mentors, you are

given advice on how to promote your abilities and manage your career. The more effectively you promote yourself the more likely you will make new contacts to add to your network.

Summary

You're the author of your career. Effective career management includes ongoing market research, self-assessment, product development and marketing your abilities and accomplishments. Networking and mentors can assist you in each of these areas. In addition, an effective network and mentors can help you succeed in your current job.

Applying the Concept

Beverly Kaye, President & Founder, Career Systems International

I think career management is easy if you truly have a passion for your chosen profession. Luckily, I do. I had two other careers, which did not hold my passion. One (short lived) as a teacher, and the other (several years) as a college dean. I fell into my current career as a management consultant (about 25 years now) while studying leadership, group dynamics, and planned change "on the side." Once I recognized that this was probably my "calling," I never stopped learning, and consequently have never tired of my work.

Networking is essential. Some of us do it naturally; some have to be taught. I do it naturally. Not only do I constantly network on behalf of my company, but I network on behalf of all my friends. I am a true believer in "what goes around, comes around." I think the key to good networking is the "quid pro quo," or the exchange of favors. (I call this "elegant currencies"!)

Mentoring, similarly, is also critical. My own philosophy here is that one must be willing to mentor many, and look for mentors continually. I also believe that mentors are not necessarily older, or more senior. Mentors can be found in the most unusual places if you know where and how to look. (My 13-year old taught me all my computer skills. My rocket scientist husband was unable to!)

I also think that self-promotion, if done well, is a necessary part of a successful career. If you don't believe in yourself, and you are not able to say so to others, why would others believe in you? As in everything else, there is a time and a place for this. An awareness of when it is "overkill" is also essential to using this ability.

Monster.com has a slogan somewhere in its advertising. It says, "Job Good, Life Good." I love that saying, and believe it is true for careers.

Applying the Concept

Thomas A. Goodrow, Vice President, for Business and Economic Development, Springfield Technical Community College

The importance of expanding your network is similar to making deposits in your bank account. They consistently add up. You can use these deposits to help you solve problems and find best practices. The more contacts I establish, the more likely I am to have the "perfect person" to help me. Whenever I attend a conference or seminar I try to introduce myself to as many people as possible.

I rely heavily on advice from my mentors. These people know what to do and how to do it. They've achieved success. In several cases, mentors have helped me shortcut a major obstacle that would have set me back or slowed my progress. I have used a variety of ways to meet with my mentor including, working out at the health club, going to lunch, attending sporting events, taking long walks, and at times, even having a beer after work at a respectable establishment. I try to stay away from the work environment so that we can distance ourselves from the pressures of daily responsibilities and be free to step back and explore new ideas without interruptions.

Every day I try to find ways to promote myself. I am not speaking of shameless self-promotion, but rather, a positive and consistent approach to communicating my vision, beliefs and talents. In this way when opportunity strikes, the appropriate decision-makers are aware of my abilities and accomplishments.

Your career is a big investment. Career choices effect you every working day. When you invest in yourself through networking, utilizing mentors and self-promotion you will generate a robust return. You'll achieve your career goals.

Bibliography

Brown, T. "How to Cut the Cost of Conflict." mgeneral.com web site.

Gallwey, W. T. *The Inner Game of Work.* 1st ed. New York: Random House, 2000.

Handy, C. *21 Ideas for Managers.* 1st ed. San Francisco, CA: Jossey-Bass Inc., 2000.

Hersey, P. and Blanchard, K. *Management of Organizational Behavior.* 4th ed. Englewood Cliffs, NJ: Prentice Hall 1982.

Krisco, K. *Leadership Your Way.* 1st ed. Alexandria, VA: Miles River Press, 1995

Kotter, J. *Leading Change.* 1st ed. Cambridge, MA: Harvard University Press, 1996.

Pfeffer, J. and Sutton, R. I., "The Smart-Talk Trap." Harvard Business Review (May-June 1999).

Schneider, D. M. and Goldwasser, C. "Be a Model Leader of Change." Management Review (March 1998).

Stevens, M. *Extreme Management.* 1st ed. New York: Warner Books, 2001.

Thornton, P. B. *Be the Leader, Make the Difference.* 1st ed. Torrance, CA: Griffin Publishing Group, 2000.

Thornton, P. B. "Teamwork: Focus, Frame, Facilitate." Management Review, (November 1992).

Tichy, Noel M., with Eli Cohen *The Leadership Engine.* 1st ed. New York: HarperCollins Publishers, 1997.

Verzuh, E. "Break it Down: A guide to Project Management." businessthinkers.com.

About the Author
Paul B. Thornton

Since 1998, Paul has been a consultant helping organizations select, train and develop outstanding leaders. His company, "**Be The Leader Associates**" (*www.betheleader.com*) offers a variety of services, seminars and workshops aimed at helping people and organizations reach their potential.

Paul has designed and conducted leadership programs for many companies including Management Development International, Kuwait Oil Corporation, and United Technologies Corporation. Since 1980 he has trained over 7,000 supervisors and managers to be more effective leaders. He's a full time faculty member at Springfield Technical Community College. The courses he teaches include Principles of Management, Leadership, Human Resource Management, Organizational Behavior, and Entrepreneurship.

For over 10 years he was manager, human resources/consultant for approximately 1,200 employees at the Hamilton Standard division of United Technologies. While at Hamilton Standard he also held the position of manager, management development and was directly involved in assessment centers, succession planning, 360 feedback, leadership reviews, and organizational restructuring.

Both in 1985 and 1996 he was the recipient of a United Technologies Award for Extraordinary Management Effectiveness. Paul is the author of numerous articles and three books focused on management and leadership. His book, *Be the Leader, Make the Difference* was selected as "one of the best business books of all time" by The CEO Refresher.

At the undergraduate level he studied psychology and political science at Ohio University. In addition, he has an M.B.A. degree from American International College and a Master of Education degree from Suffolk University.

His e-mail address is pthornton@stcc.mass.edu

HD
31
.T53

Printed in the United States
967600002BA

9 781591 130789